# Also from America's Test Kitchen

Food Gifts

Kitchen Gear

The Complete Beans and Grains Cookbook

Gatherings

A Very Chinese Cookbook

The Outdoor Cook

The Complete Modern Pantry

Everyday Bread

The Healthy Back Kitchen

The Complete Small Plates Cookbook

Fresh Pasta at Home

Desserts Illustrated

Vegan Cooking for Two

The Complete Guide to Healthy Drinks

Modern Bistro

More Mediterranean

The Complete Plant-Based Cookbook

Cooking with Plant-Based Meat

Boards

The Savory Baker

The New Cooking School Cookbook: Advanced Fundamentals

The New Cooking School Cookbook: Fundamentals

The Complete Autumn and Winter Cookbook

One-Hour Comfort

The Everyday Athlete Cookbook

Cook for Your Gut Health

Foolproof Fish

Five-Ingredient Dinners

The Ultimate Meal-Prep Cookbook

The Complete Salad Cookbook

The Chicken Bible

The Side Dish Bible

Meat Illustrated

Vegetables Illustrated

Bread Illustrated

Cooking for One

The Complete One Pot

How Can It Be Gluten-Free Cookbook Collection

The Complete Summer Cookbook

Bowls

100 Techniques

Easy Everyday Keto

Everything Chocolate

The Perfect Cookie

The Perfect Pie

The Perfect Cake

How to Cocktail

Spiced

The Ultimate Burger

The New Essentials Cookbook

Dinner Illustrated

America's Test Kitchen Menu Cookbook

Cook's Illustrated Revolutionary Recipes

Tasting Italy: A Culinary Journey

Cooking at Home with Bridget and Julia

The Complete Mediterranean Cookbook

The Complete Vegetarian Cookbook

The Complete Cooking for Two Cookbook

The Complete Diabetes Cookbook

The Complete Slow Cooker

The Complete Make-Ahead Cookbook

Just Add Sauce

How to Braise Everything

How to Roast Everything

Nutritious Delicious

What Good Cooks Know

Cook's Science

The Science of Good Cooking

Master of the Grill

Kitchen Smarts

Kitchen Hacks

100 Recipes

The New Family Cookbook

The Cook's Illustrated Baking Book

The Cook's Illustrated Cookbook

The America's Test Kitchen Family Baking Book

America's Test Kitchen Twentieth Anniversary TV Show Cookbook

The Complete America's Test Kitchen TV Show Cookbook 2001–2024

Healthy Air Fryer

Healthy and Delicious Instant Pot

Mediterranean Instant Pot

Cook It in Your Dutch Oven

Vegan for Everybody

Sous Vide for Everybody

Air Fryer Perfection

Toaster Oven Perfection

Multicooker Perfection

Food Processor Perfection

Pressure Cooker Perfection

Instant Pot Ace Blender Cookbook

Naturally Sweet

Foolproof Preserving

Paleo Perfected

The Best Mexican Recipes

Slow Cooker Revolution Volume 2: The Easy-Prep Edition

Slow Cooker Revolution

The America's Test Kitchen D.I.Y. Cookbook

**Cook's Country Titles**

Big Flavors from Italian America

One-Pan Wonders

Cook It in Cast Iron

Cook's Country Eats Local

The Complete Cook's Country TV Show Cookbook

**For a Full Listing of All Our Books**

CooksIllustrated.com

AmericasTestKitchen.com

# Praise for America's Test Kitchen Titles

"This 'very' Chinese cookbook from a father-son duo is a keeper. The book—ATK's first devoted to Chinese cooking—proves that you can teach and entertain in the same volume. . . All in all, it's one of the most charming works I've seen in years, and already want to get a second copy."

**THE WASHINGTON POST** ON *A VERY CHINESE COOKBOOK*

A Best Cookbook of 2023

**NEW YORK TIMES** ON *A VERY CHINESE COOKBOOK*

"An exhaustive but approachable primer for those looking for a 'flexible' diet. Chock-full of tips, you can dive into the science of plant-based cooking or just sit back and enjoy the 500 recipes."

**MINNEAPOLIS STAR TRIBUNE** ON *THE COMPLETE PLANT-BASED COOKBOOK*

"A mood board for one's food board is served up in this excellent guide . . . This has instant classic written all over it."

**PUBLISHERS WEEKLY** (STARRED REVIEW) ON *BOARDS: STYLISH SPREADS FOR CASUAL GATHERINGS*

Best Overall Mediterranean Cookbook 2022

**RUNNER'S WORLD** ON *THE COMPLETE MEDITERRANEAN COOKBOOK*

"Reassuringly hefty and comprehensive, *The Complete Autumn and Winter Cookbook* by America's Test Kitchen has you covered with a seemingly endless array of seasonal fare . . . This overstuffed compendium is guaranteed to warm you from the inside out."

**NPR** ON *THE COMPLETE AUTUMN AND WINTER COOKBOOK*

"Here are the words just about any vegan would be happy to read: 'Why This Recipe Works.' Fans of America's Test Kitchen are used to seeing the phrase, and now it applies to the growing collection of plant-based creations in *Vegan for Everybody*."

**THE WASHINGTON POST** ON *VEGAN FOR EVERYBODY*

"Another flawless entry in the America's Test Kitchen canon, *Bowls* guides readers of all culinary skill levels in composing one-bowl meals from a variety of cuisines."

**BUZZFEED BOOKS** ON *BOWLS*

"This comprehensive guide is packed with delicious recipes and fun menu ideas but its unique draw is the personal narrative and knowledge-sharing of each ATK chef, which will make this a hit."

**BOOKLIST** ON *GATHERINGS*

"The book's depth, breadth, and practicality makes it a must-have for seafood lovers."

**PUBLISHERS WEEKLY** (STARRED REVIEW) ON *FOOLPROOF FISH*

"*The Perfect Cookie* . . . is, in a word, perfect. This is an important and substantial cookbook . . . If you love cookies, but have been a tad shy to bake on your own, all your fears will be dissipated. This is one book you can use for years with magnificently happy results."

**HUFFPOST** ON *THE PERFECT COOKIE*

"The book offers an impressive education for curious cake makers, new and experienced alike. A summation of 25 years of cake making at ATK, there are cakes for every taste."

**THE WALL STREET JOURNAL** ON *THE PERFECT CAKE*

"The go-to gift book for newlyweds, small families, or empty nesters."

**ORLANDO SENTINEL** ON *THE COMPLETE COOKING FOR TWO COOKBOOK*

"If you're one of the 30 million Americans with diabetes, *The Complete Diabetes Cookbook* by America's Test Kitchen belongs on your kitchen shelf."

**PARADE.COM** ON *THE COMPLETE DIABETES COOKBOOK*

"True to its name, this smart and endlessly enlightening cookbook is about as definitive as it's possible to get in the modern vegetarian realm."

**MEN'S JOURNAL** ON *THE COMPLETE VEGETARIAN COOKBOOK*

# mostly
# homemade

## Antoinette Johnson

100 Recipes to Help
You Save Time and Money
While Eating Better

AMERICA'S TEST KITCHEN

Library of Congress Cataloging-in-Publication Data

Names: Johnson, Antoinette, author.

Title: Mostly homemade : 100 recipes to help you save time and money while eating better / Antoinette Johnson.

Description: Boston, MA : America's Test Kitchen, [2024] | Includes index.

Identifiers: LCCN 2024020433 (print) | LCCN 2024020434 (ebook) | ISBN 9781954210776 (paperback) | ISBN 9781954210783 (ebook)

Subjects: LCSH: Quick and easy cooking. | Low budget cooking. | LCGFT: Cookbooks.

Classification: LCC TX833.5 .J63 2024 (print) | LCC TX833.5 (ebook) | DDC 641.5/52--dc23/eng/20240517

LC record available at https://lccn.loc.gov/2024020433

LC ebook record available at https://lccn.loc.gov/2024020434

ISBN 978-1-954210-77-6

America's Test Kitchen
21 Drydock Avenue, Boston, MA 02210

Printed in China

10 9 8 7 6 5 4 3 2 1

Distributed by Penguin Random House Publisher Services
Tel: 800.733.3000

**Pictured on Front Cover** Mustard Fried Branzino (page 62), Hoisin Chicken Lettuce Wraps (page 82), Instant Pot Barbecue Ribs (page 132), Cherry-Bourbon Trifle (page 44), Cheesy Garlic Hawaiian Rolls (page 209)

**Pictured on Back Cover** Instant Pot Quesabirria Tacos (page 130), Brazilian Lemonade (page 166), No-Churn Sweet Potato Pie Ice Cream (page 43), Weeknight Ravioli Lasagna (page 116), Coconut Green Curry Chicken Noodle Soup (page 87)

**Editorial Director, Books** Adam Kowit

**Executive Food Editor** Dan Zuccarello

**Deputy Food Editor** Stephanie Pixley

**Executive Managing Editor** Debra Hudak

**Project Editor** Valerie Cimino

**Senior Editor** Camila Chaparro

**Assistant Editor** Julia Arwine

**Test Cooks** Olivia Counter, Carmen Dongo, Hisham Hassan, Laila Ibrahim, Lawman Johnson, José Maldonado, and David Yu

**Kitchen Intern** Olivia Goldstein

**Design Director** Lindsey Timko Chandler

**Deputy Art Director** Janet Taylor

**Associate Art Director** Kylie Alexander

**Photography Director** Julie Bozzo Cote

**Senior Photography Producer** Meredith Mulcahy

**Senior Staff Photographers** Steve Klise and Daniel J. van Ackere

**Staff Photographer** Kevin White

**Additional Photography** Joseph Keller

**Featured Food Stylist** Ashley Moore

**Food Stylists** Sāsha Coleman, Joy Howard, and Chantal Lambeth

**Hair and Makeup Artists** Rose Fortuna and Sarai Martinez

**Project Manager, Books** Katie Kimmerer

**Senior Print Production Specialist** Lauren Robbins

**Production and Imaging Coordinator** Amanda Yong

**Production and Imaging Specialists** Tricia Neumyer and Dennis Noble

**Copy Editor** Cheryl Redmond

**Proofreader** Kelly Gauthier

**Indexer** Elizabeth Parson

**Chief Creative Officer** Jack Bishop

**Executive Editorial Directors** Julia Collin Davison and Bridget Lancaster

# Contents

# Welcome to America's Test Kitchen

America's Test Kitchen is where curious cooks become confident cooks. Located in Boston's Seaport District in the historic Innovation and Design Building, it features 15,000 square feet of kitchen space including multiple photography and video studios. It is the home of *Cook's Illustrated* magazine and *Cook's Country* magazine and is the workday destination for more than 60 test cooks, editors, and cookware specialists. Our mission is to empower and inspire confidence, community, and creativity in the kitchen.

Since 2022, it has also been the home of *America's Test Kitchen: The Next Generation*, the reality cooking show that airs on Amazon Prime Video in which talented home cooks from across the USA compete in the job interview of a lifetime, with the grand prize being a place in the cast of the award-winning *America's Test Kitchen* TV show.

And now you hold in your hands the debut cookbook from the first-season grand-prize winner. All of these recipes are brand-new, original dishes from the creative culinary mind of Antoinette Johnson. Some are adaptations of the dishes she created on *America's Test Kitchen: The Next Generation* as she cooked her way to winning the TV competition. The rest were developed especially for this book. All of them reflect Antoinette's creative choices, flavor palate, and culinary vision for giving reluctant or time-pressed home cooks just the encouragement they need to put down the takeout menu and pick up the nonstick skillet. Our test kitchen team worked with Antoinette along the way to make sure that these recipes are easy to follow and will succeed with a wide variety of ingredient brands and in varied home kitchens.

To see what goes on behind the scenes at America's Test Kitchen, check out our social media channels for kitchen snapshots, exclusive content, video tips, and much more. You can watch us work (in our actual test kitchen) by tuning in to *America's Test Kitchen* or *Cook's Country* on public television or on our websites. Listen to Proof, Mystery Recipe, and The Walk-In (AmericasTestKitchen.com/podcasts) to hear engaging, complex stories about people and food. Want to hone your cooking skills or finally learn how to bake—with an America's Test Kitchen test cook? Enroll in one of our online cooking classes.

However you choose to visit us, we welcome you into our kitchen, where you can stand by our side as we test our way to the best recipes in America.

facebook.com/AmericasTestKitchen
instagram.com/TestKitchen
youtube.com/AmericasTestKitchen
tiktok.com/@TestKitchen
x.com/TestKitchen
pinterest.com/TestKitchen

AmericasTestKitchen.com
CooksIllustrated.com
CooksCountry.com
OnlineCookingSchool.com

---

**Join Our Community of Recipe Testers**

Our recipe testers provide valuable feedback on recipes under development by ensuring that they are foolproof in home kitchens. Help the America's Test Kitchen book team investigate the how and why behind successful recipes from your home kitchen.

# Acknowledgments

I want to express my deepest gratitude to my family for their unwavering support, their belief in me, and their invaluable contributions toward making my culinary journey possible. Their constant calls, check-ins, and assistance in raising my daughter as a single mom have made every challenge more manageable.

I am endlessly thankful for their love and support, without which I couldn't have navigated the logistical and emotional demands of appearing on *America's Test Kitchen: The Next Generation* and pursuing my passion for cooking.

It truly takes a village to raise a child, and I'm grateful for my village, in both the past and the present, for their unwavering presence in my life.

I love y'all.

# *the mostly* homemade kitchen

# Hey there, fellow busy people!

Are you one of those individuals who recognizes that you should cook more at home but can't seem to muster up the motivation to do so? Do you find yourself too often turning to takeout because you feel you just don't have the time or the energy to prepare a meal from scratch? Well, you've come to the right place for help.

Welcome to the exciting world of cooking the mostly homemade way, where simplicity reigns supreme and culinary magic really can happen in a flash. I'm here to show you that time spent preparing food can be effortless, enjoyable, and so very rewarding, even if you currently rarely cook or even if you're a beginner who hasn't ventured much beyond boiling water.

Now, before you start rolling your eyes and reaching for that takeout menu, let me assure you that this isn't your average cookbook. This is a culinary journey mapped out specifically for those who don't have the precious hours in the day to spend in the kitchen or who don't have culinary confidence, whether through lack of practice or lack of experience. Believe me, I get it—life can be busy, even chaotic, but that should not mean sacrificing the rewards of a home-cooked meal.

In these pages, you'll find a treasure trove of fast and simple recipes that require minimal effort but deliver maximum flavor. I've developed each recipe with time constraints and taste appeal equally in mind. Think of these recipes as kitchen adventures designed to make everybody's taste buds do a happy dance, all while keeping the process wonderfully convenient. Who knows, you might even discover your inner chef.

What's the secret? Well, it lies in making the most of ingredient versatility and premade grocery items. Using a relatively small number of everyday supermarket ingredients across multiple recipes reduces food waste, makes your pantry more efficient, and stretches your shopping dollars further. No more buying obscure ingredients that you use once and then let languish in the back of your cupboard or the refrigerator door until they go bad. Likewise, with my clever hacks and creative use of prepackaged foods ranging from frozen and canned produce and refrigerated pesto to tinned fish and rotisserie chicken, you can whip up gourmet-worthy dishes without breaking a sweat.

My mostly homemade approach to cooking is the ultimate time-saving solution that ensures you'll have more minutes to savor the flavors with less time spent chopping, peeling, and dicing. Whether you're cooking for just yourself or you're feeding two or more, you'll find that these recipes are all about practicality, ease, and affordability—because great food shouldn't come at the cost of your sanity or your wallet.

So, let's roll up our sleeves, don our aprons, and dive into the delicious world of mostly homemade cooking. After a bit of exploration with this cookbook, you'll be whipping up scrumptious meals with a newfound culinary passion and a sly smile that says, "Who knew cooking could be this much fun?"

# My Story

You might be wondering how I got here—sharing my culinary journey with you through the pages of this cookbook. When I was a child, family dinners were nightly occurrences, and my mother, despite not being a fan of cooking, always had a good meal on the table. This commitment to family dinners became a cornerstone of my upbringing and a significant inspiration as I got older. I was always encouraged to be adventurous with food, and I developed a deep-seated love for eating out and trying new things.

That adventurous spirit stayed with me into adulthood. My early kitchen journey took a memorable turn when, in an attempt to impress someone, I inadvertently created "crispy shrimp quesadillas" by forgetting to remove the shrimp shells. That young-adulthood kitchen mishap fueled a determination to hone my cooking skills and never face embarrassment again.

From that moment, I embarked on a culinary exploration that found expression on Instagram. My cooking eras included a stretch of home-cooked Southern meals and a two-year plant-based era experimenting with meat replacements and vegan cheeses. The homesteading era followed, where I tried my hand at making everything from scratch. Through each phase, I acquired new techniques and sharpened my skills, gaining recognition on social media as people began requesting my full recipes and seeking out my opinions on cooking and food.

My point of view has been shaped by my traditional Southern roots; the culinary landscape of Kentucky, where I live; and the modern influence of quick home recipes. Ingredients like pulled pork, sweet potatoes, and distinct seasoning blends became integral to my cooking. Simple cooking with fresh ingredients became my mantra, and over the years, I refined my craft while documenting my culinary adventures on Instagram.

As motherhood embraced me, a new dimension of cooking came into view. It's amazing how a pint-size food critic can inspire a whole new perspective on what it means to cook with love and purpose. I found myself preparing meals not just for myself but also for my daughter, Royce. Gone were the days of "girl dinners" of cheese and jalapeño olives—clearly not toddler-approved fare! The responsibility of nourishing another human being brought a new level of intentionality to my cooking, changing how I shopped for ingredients and approached mealtime. I started crafting quick recipes that balanced nutritional value with culinary flair, while ensuring they pleased my young daughter's discerning taste buds.

Then came the turning point—my aunt shared casting information for *America's Test Kitchen: The Next Generation*, and the rest, as they say, is history. My experience on that show was life-changing. Winning was a dream come true, and the experience sparked a desire in me to evolve from a hobbyist home chef into a culinary professional.

Since winning Season 1 of *America's Test Kitchen: The Next Generation*, I've immersed myself in learning about food the ATK way, focusing on technique, consistency, and science. I've catered events overseas, showcased my skills as a featured chef for large gatherings, and proudly earned the title of family cook at all our Southern family gatherings—a significant honor.

I invite you to step into my kitchen, a place where the wisdom of my Southern roots joins with the quick, relatable tips so necessary to a busy modern life to make each recipe a shared experience that feels like home.

# The Mostly Homemade Pantry

Back when I was a fresh-faced college newbie, I felt ready to take on the world. Of course, like most people that age, I had plenty to learn, including in the kitchen. My mom taught me a lot about cooking, including her most powerful secret weapon: always having a stocked pantry. Boy, was that a game-changer! My well-stocked pantry became my best kitchen ally, leaving me feeling confident enough to tackle any cooking situation, from improvising ingredient substitutions or livening up Monday night dinners to unexpectedly entertaining friends on a weekend.

Think of your pantry as a treasure chest that you can open to create valuable jewels of condiments, sauces, dressings, seasoning blends, and more. The best part is, you don't even need to build a large or expensive pantry. Well-chosen supermarket staples can be combined in many different ways to create a host of different flavors. Here's a list of what you need to successfully cook from this book. Of course, you can add more items according to your preferences.

## Shelf-Stable

**Bourbon**

**Broth**   boxed beef broth, boxed chicken broth, vegetable broth base

**Canned beans**   cannellini, chickpeas

**Canned fruits**   blueberry and cherry pie fillings, coconut milk

**Canned and bottled tomatoes**   crushed (regular, fire roasted), diced with green chiles, paste, marinara sauce

**Canned vegetables**   artichoke hearts, carrots, chipotle chiles in adobo sauce, green chiles, sweet potato puree, unseasoned collard greens

**Dried herbs**   dill, Italian seasoning, oregano, rosemary, thyme

**Dried pasta and noodles**   linguine, penne, rice noodles

**Dried spices**   allspice, cayenne, chili powder, cinnamon, curry powder, garlic powder, ginger, Old Bay, onion powder, nutmeg, red pepper flakes, seasoned salt, smoked paprika

**Garlic, onions, and shallots**

**Honey**

**Hot sauce**   my favorite is Texas Pete

**Liquid smoke**

**Long-grain white rice**

**Molasses**

**Oils**   extra-virgin olive, toasted sesame, vegetable

**Panko bread crumbs**

**Peanut butter**

**Potato gnocchi**

**Sugars**   confectioners', dark brown, granulated

**Sweetened condensed milk**

**Tinned fish**   baby clams, crab, oysters, salmon

**Vanilla bean paste**   or vanilla extract

**Vinegars**   cider, red wine, seasoned rice

**Worcestershire sauce**

# Refrigerator

**Caramelized onion jam**

**Cheeses** cheddar, cream cheese, goat cheese (plain, garlic and herb), Monterey Jack, Parmesan, Pecorino Romano

**Citrus** lemons, limes, oranges

**Fully cooked bacon**

**Hoisin sauce**

**Ketchup**

**Mustards** Chinese hot, Dijon, yellow

**Pesto**

**Prosciutto**

**Roasted red peppers**

**Rotisserie chicken**

**Soy sauce**

**Sriracha**

**Strawberry preserves**

**Thai green curry paste**

**Wine and beer** dry Marsala, red and white wine, dark beer

# Freezer

**Bone-in chicken thighs**

**Doughs** phyllo shells, pie rounds, pizza dough, puff pastry

**Fresh ginger**

**Fruits** pineapple chunks, sliced peaches, frozen grape juice concentrate

**Ground beef** (80 percent lean)

**Homestyle mini meatballs**

**Nuts** cashews, peanuts, walnuts

**Pasta and noodles** ravioli, tortellini, fresh Chinese wheat noodles

**Sausage** andouille, bratwurst, Mexican-style chorizo

**Shrimp**

**Vegetables** butternut squash pieces; carrot, corn, and green bean medley; green peas; hash brown patties

# Grocery Store Savvy

Cooking mostly homemade goes beyond just mastering recipes; it also involves a savvy approach to grocery shopping. The familiar perimeter of the grocery store gets a lot of attention for its fresh produce, meats and dairy, and so forth, but here we celebrate the sometimes forgotten inner aisles, the hidden gems of shelf stability. Knowing how to navigate these aisles is a skill that stocks your pantry and saves you money while helping you reduce food waste. Here are some of my favorite tips for getting the most out of your grocery runs.

## Shop in bulk if you can.

Buying items in larger quantities takes advantage of economies of scale, reduces packaging costs, and sometimes offers wholesale prices—all of which gets you more value for your money. Buying in bulk also means less-frequent shopping, saving you time and transportation costs. For example, if you have the freezer space, buy large packs of bone-in chicken thighs and bags of shrimp. Large cans of extra-virgin olive oil can be great deals. Even buying larger bottles of items like hot sauce, mustard, and vinegar can save money.

## Embrace the thrill of supermarket sales.

Turn each visit to the grocery store into a treasure hunt. Let go of brand loyalty and you'll find that you can maximize value and savings by discovering new products at discounted prices. Now and then I embrace a particular brand that I love, like Texas Pete Hot Sauce for my Air-Fried Game Day Wings (page 78) and other recipes, or a brand that is hard to replace with something else, like Old Bay seasoning, but mostly I buy whatever is on sale.

## Rise and shine for a.m. grocery runs.

Stores often mark down items nearing expiration, and first thing in the morning is the best time to score these types of bargains on fresh produce, baked goods, and more. If you need motivation for early morning shopping, check out my Ginger-Orange Soda (page 165), which was inspired by a full bag of gorgeous blood oranges that I purchased for only 99 cents.

## Seek out in-season local produce.

Whether you're shopping at your local grocery store or farmers' market, buying in-season fruits and vegetables will not only let you enjoy fresher ingredients but will also save you money, as in-season items tend to be more affordable. You can make this work all year round, from buying fresh berries in the summertime for Sparkling Whipped Cream Dip with Berries (page 186) to transforming a humble green cabbage in the dead of winter into Dijon-Lemon Roasted Cabbage Wedges (page 159).

## Make the salad bar your supermarket ally.

You might think this method of shopping would be more expensive, but at the salad bar you can grab precisely what you need, from crisp greens to colorful vegetables to cooked proteins. This can be more cost-effective than ending up throwing unused fresh ingredients away, especially when you're cooking for one or two people. It even works when you need just a small amount of something fresh for any given recipe, like the small quantities of chopped bell pepper and celery needed for my Crab Salad Pastry Puffs (page 180).

## Know when it's worth it.

Some premium ingredients are worth the splurge. Extra-virgin olive oil adds depth of flavor, transforming simple dishes into gourmet delights. Tinned fish, like high-quality salmon or oysters, infuses dishes like Sriracha-Soy Salmon Sliders (page 29) and Oysters Rockefeller Dip (page 24) with savory umami punch. Vanilla bean paste—more expensive than vanilla extract but more affordable and convenient than vanilla beans— brings its rich flavor and aroma to Cherry-Bourbon Trifle (page 44) and Sweet Potato Pie Dip (page 189). And good news: Many of these premium ingredients go on sale, making them even more enticing for savvy shoppers. Keep an eye out for promotions and discounts, especially during seasonal and holiday sales.

# Become a Smart Home Cook

Becoming a smart home cook isn't about mastering complex recipes from the get-go; instead, like any habit or practice, it's about a journey of getting comfortable in the kitchen through regular cooking. I understand that this can be challenging, especially if you're pressed for time or you'd just rather be doing something other than cooking. A savvy home cook knows how to master the art of efficiency without compromising on taste. The key to this lies in embracing the process and not letting mistakes deter you. Every mishap in the kitchen is a valuable lesson in disguise. Here are some steps you can take to work smarter, not harder, in your home kitchen.

## Lean into canned and frozen produce.

In a world where time is a precious commodity, having a backup plan for fresh vegetables is a game-changer. Canned and frozen produce is just as nutritious as fresh and is almost always less expensive, so keeping your pantry stocked with a varied selection ensures a nutrient-rich addition to your meal even on the busiest nights. In chapter 1, "Maximize the Canned Aisle," I share some of my favorite recipes focusing on canned goods.

## Leverage big-flavor prepared foods.

Saving time doesn't mean sacrificing flavor. Harness the convenience of big-flavor prepared foods—think rotisserie chicken, cooked bacon, store-bought pesto, chipotle chiles in adobo, and even boxed cake mix. These kitchen heroes add loads of flavor and substance without the hassle of sourcing and preparing ingredients. Chapter 3, "Reimagine Prepared Foods," shows you how to work wonders with rotisserie chicken, prepared pesto, and more.

## Store produce properly.

It's tempting to just throw everything into the fridge when you get home from a shopping run, but a few upfront precautions will make your fresh vegetables and fruits keep longer.

**Berries**  Pick them over right after you get home to immediately remove any suspicious-looking berries. From there, you've got two options to further avoid premature spoilage. A) Wash the berries right before consumption. B) Dunk the berries into a bowl with 3 cups water and 1 cup distilled white vinegar. Rinse them in another bowl of water, then pat dry thoroughly and refrigerate.

**Leafy greens and fresh herbs**  Remove wire twist ties and store lettuce, spinach, and the like in ventilated containers or partially open produce bags in the crisper drawer with a damp paper towel tucked inside to control moisture.

**Onions, shallots, garlic, and potatoes**  Store these items in a cool, dark place with good ventilation to prevent sprouting.

**Tomatoes**  Keep at room temperature, away from direct sunlight, to preserve their flavor and texture.

# Don't forget the freezer.

If you find yourself with leftovers from recipes, consider freezing them instead of refrigerating them. These frozen "bonus meals" cut down on food spoilage and expand your dinner options on busy weeknights. Be sure to label the container with what's inside and the date you stored it. Here are some of my favorite freezer-friendly recipes.

# Become a Smart Home Cook

# Give ingredients a second life.

Before you throw something away, think creatively about how you might be able to use it. Here are some of my practices.

**Bacon grease**   I often use precooked bacon for speed and convenience, but when I do cook bacon, I reserve the fat, storing it in a jar in the refrigerator or freezer for cooking.

**Pecorino and Parmesan rinds**   Store these in the freezer and pull one out as needed to add savory depth to all manner of soups and stews.

**Pickle juice**   After the pickles are gone, repurpose that tangy juice! Mix it into salad dressings or marinades instead of vinegar for a delightful zing.

**Rotisserie chicken bones**   I'm all about getting the most out of that supermarket standby, rotisserie chicken. Simmer the carcass with water, vegetables, and herbs to create a richly flavorful homemade broth. Use it as a base for soups or a cooking liquid for grains.

**Stale bread**   Toast it until golden, then blitz it in a food processor for homemade bread crumbs that you can store in your freezer.

# Plan your weekly menu.

Now, I know that meal planning might not be your Friday night turn-on, but trust me, staying ahead of the game is the key to kitchen serenity. Whip out that planner, choose some recipes and what you'll need to buy for them, and daily dinnertime will feel less like a last-minute scramble and more like a walk in the park.

# Hit the sheets with a clean kitchen.

Last but not least, although this isn't directly food-related, trust me when I say that going to bed with a clean kitchen is the unsung hero of time-saving strategies. Wake up to a fresh start, not yesterday's dishes. A clean slate equals a smoother cooking experience and fewer excuses to not cook.

# Mostly Homemade Kitchen Gear

Don't worry—you don't need any specialty equipment to cook successfully from this book. Here's some basic everyday gear that will make your cooking go smoothly.

**Nonstick skillets**   Many of my recipes call for a 12-inch nonstick skillet, so this is what I most recommend for all-purpose use. A number of my recipes have smaller serving sizes (two or three servings, and even one serving in a few cases like Herbed Goat Cheese Scramble, page 106), so an 8-inch nonstick skillet and a 10-inch nonstick skillet are also nice to have.

**Regular skillets**   Again, a 12-inch skillet will prove itself as an all-purpose workhorse in your kitchen. Also helpful, if you have the space and the budget, are 8-inch and 10-inch regular skillets.

**Saucepans**   Small, medium, and large saucepans are must-haves for many recipes in this book.

**Large pot or Dutch oven**   Besides making cozy soups such as Tortellini Tomato Soup (page 39), this pot is useful for boiling potatoes for Spicy Potato Salad with Honey-Chipotle Dressing (page 52) and noodles for Mustard-Sesame Noodles (page 93).

**Rimmed baking sheets**   These will let you make fun apps and party food like Mini Chicken Pot Pies (page 96) and Pesto-Stuffed Mushrooms (page 104) as well as hearty weeknight meals including Not Your Mother's Meatloaf (page 147). I have an assortment of sizes, but an 18 by 13-inch rimmed sheet is the most versatile choice.

**8-inch square baking pan**   This gets you to awesome fast dinners including Weeknight Ravioli Lasagna (page 116) and Oven-Roasted Smothered Chicken Thighs (page 142).

**13 by 9-inch baking pan**   A larger pan helps you feed a crowd with Overnight Breakfast Casserole (page 194) or Lemon-Blueberry Dump Crumble (page 210).

**9-inch pie plate**   You'll want this to make Bacon–Green Chile Quiche (page 154).

**Muffin tin**   Either a 6-cup or a 12-cup standard-size tin will let you make Mini Carbonara Quiche Cups (page 156).

**Mixer**   If you have a stand mixer, feel free to use it (it will make for easier prep for the Sparkling Whipped Cream Dip with Berries on page 186), but for all of my recipes that call for a mixer, a hand mixer will work fine.

**Blender or food processor**   Use either to whip up a quick, sophisticated sauce for Crispy Gnocchi with Roasted Red Pepper Sauce (page 115). And I hope that my version of Brazilian Lemonade (page 166) rocks your world as much as it rocked mine.

In addition to these tools, there are two countertop appliances that are integral to my home cooking because of their time-saving capabilities and their amazing convenience, and owning them will help you truly make the most of this book.

## Air Fryer

Essentially miniature convection ovens, air fryers don't actually fry your food. Their powerful fans circulate hot air around the food to create crisp crusts and juicy interiors using only a little oil. Preheating time is minimal, and cooking times are typically faster than traditional convection ovens, making the air fryer a hero for fast weeknight dinners. I rely on mine to make Air-Fried Pesto Salmon Fillet (page 103), Air-Fried Crispy Gnocchi with Artichokes (page 112), and Air-Fried Chicken Tenders with Chipotle Mayo (page 73), among other dishes. The test kitchen's favorite is the Instant Vortex Plus 6-Quart Air Fryer. It is compact in size but fits enough food for four people. It's user-friendly, and the nonstick interior is a cinch to clean. If you want a smaller air fryer that cooks enough food for two people, the test kitchen recommends the Philips Premium Airfryer with Fat Removal Technology.

## Instant Pot

I love my Instant Pot so much that I have an entire chapter of recipes (starting on page 121) devoted to this appliance, which can pressure-cook, slow-cook, sear and sauté, and more. My favorite way to use it is to transform traditionally long-cooking recipes into dishes that I like to call Wednesday-night ready. The Instant Pot allows me to make the Southern-style classic dishes I grew up eating, including collard greens (see page 139) and an Eastern Carolina pulled pork (see page 135) inspired by my grandpa, in a fraction of the time that it would take otherwise, without sacrificing anything in the way of flavor. I also use it to make a beef ragu (see page 129) that tastes like it simmered all day and a simplified adaptation of Cajun shrimp and rice (see page 136). The test kitchen's favorite multicooker is the Instant Pot Pro 8Qt. The Instant Pot Pro 6Qt is the smaller recommended size.

# Practice Culinary Flexibility

Once you find yourself hitting your culinary stride, it's time to ditch the training wheels and embrace a higher level of kitchen wizardry. Being a good home cook is about more than just following recipes—it's a dynamic dance where you lead and the ingredients follow. It's about thinking strategically, improvising fearlessly, and substituting confidently. As you become more comfortable, the kitchen will become your playground, with every dish an opportunity to flex your creative culinary muscles.

## *Cross-utilize ingredients.*

I don't buy condiments without knowing how I'm going to use them up or store them for longevity. For example, I use Thai green curry paste in Curry-Braised Chicken Leg Quarters (page 74) and then again in Coconut Green Curry Chicken Noodle Soup (page 87). Or I might just thin the leftover paste with canned coconut milk and toss it with cooked noodles. I use chipotle chiles in adobo sauce in Spicy Potato Salad with Honey-Chipotle Dressing (page 52) or Chicken Enchilada Bake (page 95) and then freeze the leftover chiles in tablespoon-size dollops, ready for plucking from the freezer when needed.

## *Make smart substitutions.*

When you run out of specific ingredients or don't want to make a grocery run for just one item, don't be afraid to make substitutions based on what you have on hand. My go-to tortellini is the frozen variety, but if you only have the shelf-stable variety, go for it. I love the flavor, aroma, and color that vanilla bean paste brings to recipes, but if you only have vanilla extract, you can just sub in an equal amount. Your family doesn't do ground beef? Sub in 93 percent lean ground turkey. Sour cream and Greek yogurt are interchangeable in most recipes; you could even use cream cheese loosened with a tablespoon or two of milk or water. These types of smart, low-risk substitutions will help you get really comfortable in the kitchen.

# *Practice improvisation.*

This naturally follows from making smart substitutions and will make you feel like a culinary wizard. I love playing with flavor profiles by using the same or similar ingredients in different proportions or making a versatile sauce that goes with many different foods. With a little experimentation, you can create distinctively different dishes from the same basic ingredients. For example:

**Chinese hot mustard**   For the Hot Honey Mustard–Peanut Dressing (page 48), adding honey and peanut butter balances the clean heat of the mustard with nutty sweetness. For the Mustard-Sesame Noodles (page 93), start again with Chinese hot mustard as the anchor, but this time add toasted sesame oil for richness and rice vinegar for a balancing acidity.

**Strawberry preserves**   Combined with soy sauce, red wine vinegar, and red pepper flakes, the unlikely ingredient of strawberry preserves creates a bright and spicy glaze for Hot Pepper–Strawberry Wings (page 77). Or mix the preserves with hoisin sauce to make a sweet-salty, umami-rich sauce for Strawberry-Hoisin Meatballs (page 196).

**A simple, versatile sauce**   The sauce in the Brown Sugar–Soy Sauce Stir-Fry (page 57) works well with just about any frozen vegetable you like. The Honey-Chipotle Dressing for the Spicy Potato Salad (page 52) is delicious drizzled over broiled chicken or shrimp. And the Fried Food Sauce (page 61)—well, that's pretty great with anything fried!

# Rescue Your Produce

Despite all the best intentions, it's easy to let delicate fresh produce disintegrate in the fridge after you've used a small amount for a specific recipe. Fresh herb bunches turn to mush in the blink of an eye, and don't get me started on the short life of fresh berries. To prevent food waste and make the most of these flavorful but more perishable ingredients, I came up with some creative recipes for rescuing them before they turn into something you wouldn't want to eat. You can think of each of these recipes as a template: Adjust the choice or proportions of the herbs, vegetables, or fruits in each recipe according to what you need to use up.

## Pesto Sauce

**Makes:** ½ cup · **Total time:** 25 minutes

*I use pesto frequently in my cooking, as you'll see throughout the recipes in this book. I typically purchase prepared refrigerated pesto, but when I have fresh herbs on hand, it's a treat to make my own. This amount is just right to sauce 8 ounces of pasta—though I've also been known to just slather it on crusty bread and call it a meal. This recipe can be easily scaled down or up to accommodate whatever quantity of herbs you have on hand. You can vary the proportions of the basil and parsley as well, if you have more or less of one of the herbs.*

|   |   |
|---|---|
| 1 | garlic clove, unpeeled |
| 1½ | teaspoons pine nuts |
| ⅔ | cup minced fresh basil |
| ⅓ | cup minced fresh parsley |
| 3 | tablespoons grated Pecorino Romano cheese |
| ⅛ | teaspoon table salt |
| ⅓ | cup extra-virgin olive oil |

**1** Toast garlic in 8-inch skillet over medium heat, shaking skillet occasionally, until softened and spotty brown, about 8 minutes. When garlic is cool enough to handle, remove and discard skin, and mince. Meanwhile, toast pine nuts in now-empty skillet over medium heat, stirring often, until golden and fragrant, 4 to 5 minutes. Remove from skillet and let cool, then chop pine nuts fine and combine with garlic in medium bowl.

**2** Stir basil, parsley, Pecorino, and salt into garlic mixture in bowl. While whisking constantly, slowly drizzle oil into herb mixture until combined. Serve. (Pesto can be refrigerated for up to 3 days. To prevent browning, press plastic wrap flush to surface or top with thin layer of olive oil. Bring to room temperature before using.)

# Chimichurri

**Makes:** 1 cup · **Total time:** 10 minutes

Bright, tangy, garlicky chimichurri is an Argentinian classic, often served alongside grilled meat. As its popularity has grown throughout Latin America and beyond, many variations have emerged. I like my version with The Perfect Steak (page 65) or Air-Fried Chicken Tenders (page 73). As long as you have 1½ cups herbs total, this sauce will come together just fine. Or you can easily halve this recipe if you don't have enough herbs; if you do that, use a blender instead of a food processor to ensure even blending.

| | |
|---|---|
| 1 | cup fresh parsley leaves |
| ½ | cup fresh cilantro leaves |
| 2 | tablespoon red wine vinegar |
| 4 | garlic cloves, minced |
| 1 | teaspoon table salt |
| ¼ | teaspoon pepper |
| ⅔ | cup extra-virgin olive oil |

Pulse parsley, cilantro, vinegar, garlic, salt, and pepper in food processor until finely chopped, about 20 pulses, scraping down sides of processor bowl as needed. With processor running, slowly drizzle in oil until well combined. Serve. (Chimichurri can be refrigerated for up to 3 days.)

# Pickled Vegetables

**Makes:** about 3 cups

**Total time:** 15 minutes, plus 3½ hours cooling

This is a fabulous way to transform fresh vegetables that have been lingering in your produce drawer into a punchy topping for sandwiches or burgers. They are also a must to serve with Instant Pot Barbecue Burnt Ends (page 125). You can substitute 8 ounces halved or quartered white mushrooms, thinly sliced peppers (hot or sweet), or quartered radishes for the cucumber. Whatever vegetable you use in this speedy pickle will stay pretty crunchy due to the short brining time. I use a Mason jar, but you can use any container (or split the batch among multiple containers) to pickle the vegetables, as long as they are fully submerged in the brine. Using a funnel and ladle is the most efficient and safest way to pour the hot brine into the jar.

| | |
|---|---|
| 1 | (12-ounce) English cucumber, sliced ½ inch thick |
| 3 | sprigs fresh dill |
| 1½ | cups cider vinegar |
| ¼ | cup water |
| 2 | tablespoons sugar |
| 1½ | teaspoons kosher salt |
| ½ | teaspoon black peppercorns |

**1** Place one 1-quart jar under hot running water until heated through, about 1 minute; shake dry. Pack cucumber and dill into hot jar.

**2** Bring vinegar, water, sugar, salt, and peppercorns to boil in medium saucepan over medium-high heat. Using funnel and ladle, pour hot brine over cucumber to cover. Let jar cool to room temperature, about 30 minutes.

**3** Cover jar with lid and refrigerate for at least 3 hours before serving. (Pickles can be refrigerated for up to 1 week.)

# Rescue Your Produce

## Berry Coulis

**Makes:** about 1 cup   ·   **Total time:** 15 minutes

*A coulis sounds like a fancy restaurant menu item, but it's really just a simple cooked sauce that has been strained to give it a smooth texture. Fruits are often used to make a sweet coulis, though there are also savory versions made with vegetables. This coulis can be made using any combination of berries or just a single berry, and you can halve the recipe if you have fewer leftover berries in your fridge. It will dress up any store-bought ice cream or pound cake enough to really impress friends and family. It's not just for dessert, though—I sometimes stir it into yogurt for breakfast!*

| | |
|---|---|
| 12 | ounces blueberries, blackberries, raspberries, or halved strawberries (2½ cups) |
| ½ | cup sugar |
| ¼ | cup orange juice |
| | Pinch table salt |

**1**    Combine all ingredients in small saucepan. Cook over medium heat, stirring occasionally, until berries are broken down and sauce is thickened slightly, about 10 minutes for raspberries, 15 minutes for blueberries, or 18 minutes for blackberries or strawberries. (Strawberries will not completely break down during cooking.)

**2**    Process sauce in blender until smooth, about 30 seconds. Strain through fine-mesh strainer into bowl; discard solids. Let cool to desired temperature, then serve. (Sauce can be refrigerated for up to 1 week.)

## Simmer Pot

**Total time:** 20 minutes

*Scented candles are insanely expensive and are often made using artificial scents and other ingredients I don't really want to inhale. Here's an alternative that is all-natural, sustainable, and extremely cost-effective. By replenishing the water, you can maintain the simmer pot over the course of several hours. I love this vanilla-lime-rosemary combination; instead of the vanilla extract, you can use a spent vanilla bean pod after you've used the seeds for another recipe. Other combos I like include almond extract with orange slices and whole cloves, lemon extract with lemon slices and thyme sprigs, and mint extract with apple slices or apple peels. Experiment to find your own personalized scent!*

| | |
|---|---|
| 3 | quarts water |
| 2 | tablespoons vanilla extract |
| 4 | limes, sliced into thin rounds |
| 4 | sprigs fresh rosemary |

Combine all ingredients in large saucepan. Bring to boil over high heat, then reduce heat to low to maintain gentle simmer. As water evaporates, add additional water as desired.

# Chapter 1

## Maximize the Canned Aisle

Oysters Rockefeller Dip

Smoked Salmon Dip

Sriracha-Soy Salmon Sliders

Linguine with Baby Clams

Beer Brat Pasta

Weeknight Collard Greens

Ginger-Miso Carrots

Tortellini Tomato Soup

Sweet Potato Soufflé

No-Churn Sweet Potato Pie Ice Cream

Cherry-Bourbon Trifle

# Oysters Rockefeller Dip

**Serves:** 4 to 6　·　**Total time:** 20 minutes

*While it's safe to say that kale has probably had the most successful food rebrand of all time, canned fish—now going by the fancier name tinned fish—has gained plenty of ground as a chic trend. Cooks across the socials are appreciating this shelf-stable ingredient and realizing the flavor it can pack into so many different dishes. I hope this trend is here to stay, and to kick off a few of my favorite tinned fish recipes, I'm starting with the one that made Ms. Elle Simone Scott herself tell me on camera for all to hear, "You can cook." My dad and I like to enjoy smoked tinned oysters right out of the can with crackers and hot sauce, what I call "poor man's oysters on the half shell." But even better is this luscious, creamy, warm dip made with smoked oysters, which pairs perfectly with hearty crackers or crusty bread. When I made this dish for the first time on America's Test Kitchen: The Next Generation, my immediate impulse was to use the fresh oysters available to us in the pantry. After spending precious minutes attempting to shuck them, I pivoted, thinking I could save time and incorporate more flavor with smoked oysters—and boy, was I right! This recipe can be easily doubled.*

1 tablespoon unsalted butter

1 small shallot, minced

2 garlic cloves, minced

1 tablespoon all-purpose flour

1 cup heavy cream

1 (3.75-ounce) can smoked oysters, drained with juice reserved, oysters chopped fine

¼ teaspoon table salt

½ cup finely chopped baby spinach

1 tablespoon chopped fresh parsley

1 teaspoon lemon juice

Sliced baguette or crackers

**1**　Melt butter in small saucepan over medium heat. Add shallot and cook until softened, about 3 minutes. Stir in garlic and cook until fragrant, about 30 seconds. Stir in flour and cook for 1 minute.

**2**　Whisk in cream until well combined, then stir in oysters and reserved juice and salt. Bring to simmer, then reduce heat to medium-low. Stir in spinach and simmer until spinach is wilted, about 3 minutes. Stir in parsley and lemon juice and season with salt and pepper to taste. Serve hot with sliced baguette or crackers.

## *Pantry Pick*

**Smoked tinned oysters:** If smoked tinned oysters are new to you, imagine a flavor-packed bite that's the perfect balance of salty and smoky. Plus, they are rich in omega-3 fatty acids. There are lots of good brands out there; for this recipe, look for one that's packed in oil and specifies that the oysters are smoked using natural hardwood.

# Smoked Salmon Dip

**Serves:** 8 · **Total time:** 15 minutes

*When working with canned ingredients, it's important to incorporate some fresh elements, along with some ingredients that can add flavor depth. Plenty of lemon, some fresh herbs, and a bit of zesty seafood seasoning combine here to amp up canned salmon. And, since there's also something about the smoky flavor of food cooked on a grill that will always bring an immediate yes from me, I often like to add a dash of liquid smoke to indoor recipes to give them a complex smoky flavor. When creating this recipe, I was a bit shocked to find out that canned salmon was not a staple in other people's households like it is in mine. Salmon croquettes made using canned salmon were a regular menu item when I was growing up, and they were always my favorite.*

1 (15-ounce) can salmon, drained and picked over for large bones

8 ounces cream cheese, cut into 8 pieces and softened

2 scallions, sliced thin

1 tablespoon grated lemon zest plus 3 tablespoons juice

1 teaspoon chopped fresh dill, plus extra for garnish

1 teaspoon table salt

¾ teaspoon liquid smoke

½ teaspoon Old Bay seasoning

½ teaspoon pepper

Sliced baguette or crackers

Mix salmon, cream cheese, scallions, lemon zest and juice, dill, salt, liquid smoke, Old Bay, and pepper in bowl until well combined. Garnish with extra dill and serve with sliced baguette or crackers. (Dip can be refrigerated in airtight container for up to 24 hours.)

## *Pantry Picks*

**Canned salmon:** Several species of salmon are available in cans. Pink salmon is the most reasonably priced, though if you want to splash out you could buy sockeye salmon. For cooking, I buy water-packed salmon. You'll see that the fish bones are still present in canned salmon. The canning process makes the bones very soft and perfectly safe to eat (and they contain calcium!). I often don't bother picking them out, but you can do that if you prefer.

**Liquid smoke:** Made from the condensed smoke of burned firewood, liquid smoke is an all-natural flavoring agent. If you want to give the illusion that you broke out the hickory, reach for this, but use it sparingly, as it is potent. The test kitchen's favorite is Wright's Liquid Smoke.

## Antoinette's Tip

The slider mixture will feel very wet initially, but it will firm up nicely once you put the patties in the skillet. That's why you cook them without moving them for a minute before "smashing" them.

# Sriracha-Soy Salmon Sliders

**Serves:** 4 (makes 8 sliders)  ·  **Total time:** 35 minutes

*I think that canned salmon is the most versatile tinned fish, since it easily can be transformed to take on just about any flavor profile. I love having a few cans in my pantry so that I can still make great meals on nights when I didn't thaw any protein ahead of time or I don't have time to get to the grocery store. In fact, this is a great go-to recipe whenever you're short on time, since the sliders come together quickly and are packed with flavor. The soy sauce and brown sugar provide a salty and sweet balance that pairs perfectly with the spicy sriracha mayo. I like to add freshness and texture to the sliders by topping them with sliced tomato and lettuce. Torn Bibb or leaf lettuce works well for these sliders, but you can use whatever you prefer.*

1½ tablespoons sriracha, divided

4 teaspoons mayonnaise

2 large eggs, lightly beaten

3 tablespoons panko bread crumbs

1 tablespoon soy sauce

2 teaspoons packed dark brown sugar

1 scallion, minced

¼ teaspoon garlic powder

¼ teaspoon onion powder

1 (15-ounce) can salmon, drained and picked over for large bones

2 tablespoons extra-virgin olive oil, divided

8 slider buns, toasted if desired

1 tomato, sliced thin

Torn or shredded lettuce

**1** Combine 4 teaspoons sriracha and mayonnaise in bowl; set aside until ready to serve. Stir eggs, panko, soy sauce, sugar, scallion, garlic powder, onion powder, and remaining ½ teaspoon sriracha in bowl until well combined. Stir in salmon until well combined and cohesive.

**2** Use ¼-cup measure to divide salmon mixture into 8 equal portions. Heat 1 tablespoon oil in 12-inch nonstick skillet over medium-high heat until shimmering. Add 4 salmon portions to skillet and cook for 1 minute without moving, then use spatula to press each portion into 3-inch-wide patty. Continue to cook until well browned and crispy on both sides, 5 to 7 minutes, flipping gently using 2 spatulas. Transfer to large plate and repeat with remaining 1 tablespoon oil and remaining 4 salmon portions.

**3** Serve salmon sliders on buns with reserved sriracha mayo, tomato, and lettuce.

## *Pantry Pick*

**Sriracha:** This Thai-style chili sauce went viral in America around 2010, and not a moment too soon. Its garlicky, sweet-yet-fiery flavor and thick texture adds zip to dishes from noodles and rice to eggs to these sliders. The test kitchen's favorite is Kikkoman Sriracha Hot Chile Sauce.

# Linguine with Baby Clams

**Serves:** 2 · **Total time:** 40 minutes

*Canned clam linguine: Can it compare to fresh? Only if you follow this recipe, lol. To win the second challenge on America's Test Kitchen: The Next Generation, I created a recipe for panko-crusted broiled fresh clams over linguine with fresh clam sauce. It's a really fun and unexpected dish, but it's definitely not what I would call "Wednesday night–ready." These are the dishes that I can make in 30 to 45 minutes during a busy weeknight and that don't require a lot of pot-and-pan cleanup. This weeknight-friendly dish incorporates shallot, garlic, fresh parsley, lemon, and just a small amount of fresh tomato to add brightness to tender tinned baby clams. The butter stirred in at the end adds wonderful richness. Now, I know that you can buy ready-made clam sauce in a can or a jar, but I would make this fresh-tasting, no-fuss recipe over using those products every time. This recipe can be easily doubled.*

| | |
|---|---|
| 8 | ounces linguine |
| ½ | teaspoon table salt, plus salt for cooking pasta |
| 1 | tablespoon extra-virgin olive oil |
| 1 | small shallot, minced |
| 2 | garlic cloves, minced |
| ⅛ | teaspoon red pepper flakes |
| 1 | (10-ounce) can baby clams, drained |
| 2 | Campari tomatoes, stemmed and chopped |
| 1½ | tablespoons lemon juice |
| 4 | tablespoons unsalted butter, cut into 4 pieces |
| 2 | tablespoons chopped fresh parsley |

**1** Bring 2 quarts water to boil in large saucepan. Add pasta and 1½ teaspoons salt and cook, stirring often, until al dente. Reserve ½ cup cooking water, then drain pasta and set aside.

**2** Meanwhile, heat oil in 12-inch nonstick skillet over medium heat until shimmering. Add shallot and cook until softened, about 3 minutes. Stir in garlic and pepper flakes and cook until fragrant, about 30 seconds. Add clams, tomatoes, lemon juice, and salt; increase heat to medium-high; and cook for 1 minute.

**3** Off heat, add reserved pasta to sauce in skillet and toss to combine. Stir in butter pieces and toss with pasta until melted. Adjust consistency of sauce with reserved cooking water as needed, then stir in parsley and season with pepper to taste. Serve.

## *Pantry Pick*

**Canned baby clams:** Canned clams have a tender texture and sweet flavor; plus, they're a huge timesaver over fresh. They come packed in water, which I drain here to prevent the sauce from being too watery. You can use chopped clams instead, though your finished dish won't be as pretty.

### Antoinette's Tip

You want the fresh tomatoes to stay nice and chunky and not really break down that much in the sauce. I like Campari tomatoes here because they are firm yet juicy and have a nice tangy flavor, but you can also use plum or Roma tomatoes.

# Beer Brat Pasta

**Serves:** 2  ·  **Total time:** 25 minutes

*The star of this recipe is . . . a can of beer (OK, or maybe a bottle). Sounds crazy, but hear me out. This dish leans on beer and Worcestershire sauce to anchor the flavor. By reducing them down, you create a complex sauce that doesn't take forever to make. I got the inspiration for this from a recipe in Tonya Holland's Brown Sugar Kitchen cookbook. Not to give too much away, but she reduces beer and Worcestershire sauce to create a base for one of the best versions of shrimp creole that I have ever tasted. Adding cream to this reduction creates a savory sauce that tastes as if many more ingredients were actually used. Ever since trying her recipe, I have experimented with this trifecta, using it to make amazing gravies and sauces. Here, I've also incorporated shallots along with the brats. I love how this pasta transforms the bratwurst, elevating the sausage out of its typical comfort zone of sub rolls and mustard. This recipe can be easily doubled.*

| | |
|---|---|
| 8 | ounces linguine |
| | Table salt for cooking pasta |
| 1 | tablespoon extra-virgin olive oil |
| 12 | ounces bratwurst, casings removed |
| 2 | shallots, sliced thin |
| 1 | cup dark beer |
| ½ | cup Worcestershire sauce |
| ½ | cup heavy cream |
| 1 | tablespoon chopped fresh chives |

**1**  Bring 2 quarts water to boil in large pot. Add pasta and 1½ teaspoons salt and cook, stirring often, until al dente. Reserve ½ cup cooking water, then drain pasta and set aside.

**2**  Meanwhile, heat oil in 12-inch skillet over medium heat until shimmering. Add bratwurst and cook until browned, breaking up meat with wooden spoon, 4 to 6 minutes. Transfer bratwurst to bowl.

**3**  Add shallots to fat left in skillet and cook until softened, about 3 minutes. Add beer and Worcestershire and cook for 1 minute, scraping up any browned bits. Stir in cream and reserved sausage; reduce heat to medium-low; and cook until sauce is reduced slightly, about 10 minutes.

**4**  Off heat, stir in reserved pasta, tossing to combine. Season with salt and pepper to taste and adjust consistency with reserved pasta water as needed. Sprinkle with chives and serve.

## Pantry Pick

**Beer:** The dark beer adds a rich, earthy flavor to this sauce and a slight bit of sweetness that works really well with the cream. I used Yuengling Black & Tan when developing this recipe, but you could use a dark lager, a dunkel-style beer, or a brown ale.

### Antoinette's Tip

This isn't meant to be a superclingy sauce, but after reducing, it should be thick enough to coat the back of the spoon.

# Weeknight Collard Greens

**Serves:** 6 · **Total time:** 40 minutes

*I have three go-to recipes for collard greens: this weeknight version using convenient canned collards; an Instant Pot version using fresh greens (see page 139); and my secret recipe, which I'll never share. This one is for when you're craving braised collards but need to get them done fast. By using some of my favorite pantry staples, including Worcestershire sauce, vegetable broth base, and precooked bacon, I'm able to give the canned greens the hug they need. I purchase plain unseasoned collards for this recipe, because the preseasoned canned collards are too salty and don't have much in the way of smoky depth. Bourbon is one of my favorite spirits to cook with, and when combined with the chopped bacon, it contributes the dynamic smokiness I'm looking for. The layered flavors make it seem like these greens have braised on the stove for hours.*

2  (14-ounce) cans chopped collard greens, undrained

8  slices fully cooked bacon, chopped fine

¼  cup bourbon

¼  cup cider vinegar

2  tablespoons packed dark brown sugar

2  tablespoons Worcestershire sauce

1  teaspoon garlic powder

1  teaspoon onion powder

1  teaspoon table salt

1  teaspoon vegetable broth base

¼  teaspoon paprika

Combine all ingredients in medium saucepan. Bring to simmer over medium heat and cook, adjusting heat as needed to maintain gentle simmer and stirring occasionally, until flavors meld, about 30 minutes. Serve.

## *Pantry Picks*

**Cooked bacon:** Though you can cook your own if preferred, I always keep this timesaver in my fridge for a fast way to add a touch of meaty, salty smokiness wherever it's needed. You'll find fully cooked bacon near the deli section in your grocery store.

**Vegetable broth base:** This staple adds a punch of savory flavor to vegetable dishes, soups and stews, and more, without adding a lot of liquid. Different brands of vegetable broth base can taste really different from each other, so make sure you find one you like before using it in a recipe. I used Better Than Bouillon Vegetable Base, one of the test kitchen's favorites, when developing this recipe.

# Ginger-Miso Carrots

**Serves:** 4  ·  **Total time:** 20 minutes

*Let's talk about a pantry ingredient that was new to me not long ago and that I now can't get enough of: white miso. Now of course I've tasted miso before, and I understand the flavor, but keeping it in my fridge and using it in my cooking was something I never even thought of before competing on America's Test Kitchen: The Next Generation. During the task challenge in the second episode, I was supposed to re-create a signature America's Test Kitchen recipe—a corn side dish—just by tasting it, but I couldn't figure out the source of its savory flavor. Once I learned that the dish was Miso Honey Butter Corn and the mystery flavor was from miso, I went back to my home kitchen and started experimenting with miso in everything. Because the miso is so savory, it pairs magnificently with the sweetness of carrots. This dish is versatile and perfect for those nights when you have a meat and starch picked out for dinner but can't decide on a vegetable pairing. The convenient canned carrots need only to be warmed in the delightfully sticky ginger-miso glaze.*

⅓  cup water

¼  cup packed dark brown sugar

2  tablespoons soy sauce

1  teaspoon white miso

½  teaspoon garlic powder

½  teaspoon grated fresh ginger

1  (15-ounce) can whole baby carrots, drained

**1** Combine water, sugar, and soy sauce in 10-inch nonstick skillet. Cook over medium heat, whisking frequently, until sugar is dissolved, about 2 minutes.

**2** Whisk in miso and garlic powder and cook until liquid is thick and syrupy, about 5 minutes. Off heat, whisk in ginger; transfer glaze to small bowl.

**3** Add carrots to now-empty skillet and cook over medium heat until carrots are just beginning to brown, 3 to 5 minutes. Return glaze to skillet with carrots and toss to coat. Serve.

## Antoinette's Tip

You won't get much browning on the carrots because they cook so fast, but don't worry about it, since the carrots will be nicely coated with the glossy sauce.

# Tortellini Tomato Soup

**Serves:** 6 as a main or 10 as a side  ·  **Total time:** 25 minutes

*This is tomato soup just the way I like it: hearty and packed with juicy chunks of canned crushed tomato, with the perfect combination of sweet and tart tomato flavor. By utilizing bold ingredients like red wine, Parmesan cheese, and a whopping six cloves of garlic, it's easy to create a hits-the-spot soup that tastes like it took all day to prepare (but really took less than half an hour). For this recipe, you'll also be taking a trip down my other favorite grocery store aisle—the frozen foods aisle—for cheese tortellini. You can add this pantry staple to the soup directly from the freezer—no need to thaw it first. Adding grated Parmesan at the same time as the tortellini gives the cheese time to melt into and enrich the soup.*

| | |
|---|---|
| 2 | tablespoons extra-virgin olive oil |
| 2 | large shallots, minced |
| 6 | garlic cloves, minced |
| 2 | (28-ounce) cans crushed tomatoes |
| 1 | cup chicken broth |
| ½ | cup dry red wine |
| 2 | teaspoons table salt |
| 1 | (18-ounce) bag frozen cheese tortellini |
| 3 | ounces Parmesan cheese, grated (1½ cups), plus extra for serving |
| 2 | tablespoons shredded fresh basil |

**1**  Heat oil in Dutch oven over medium heat until shimmering. Add shallots and cook until softened, about 3 minutes. Stir in garlic and cook until fragrant, about 30 seconds. Stir in tomatoes, broth, wine, and salt and bring to boil over high heat.

**2**  Stir in tortellini and Parmesan, reduce heat to medium, and return to simmer. Cook until pasta is tender, 3 to 4 minutes.

**3**  Stir in basil and season with salt and pepper to taste. Serve with extra Parmesan.

## *Pantry Picks*

### Canned crushed tomatoes:
Canned crushed tomatoes are a must-have in any respectable pantry. You can use them for sauces, pizza, stews, chilis, and quick soups like this one. There are plenty of good brands out there; the test kitchen's favorite is San Merican Crushed Tomatoes.

### Frozen cheese tortellini: I generally
prefer the texture and flavor of frozen tortellini over the shelf-stable kind. Plus, frozen tortellini typically cooks in less than half the time of the shelf-stable variety!

# Sweet Potato Soufflé

**Serves:** 6 to 8 · **Total time:** 50 minutes

*Being from the South, I love a good sweet potato dish. Growing up, I ate lots of sweet potatoes prepared in a rich and decadent way using sticks of butter, dark brown sugar, and white sugar. Sometimes they were mashed, sometimes they were sliced, but the common denominator was that they were always supersweet and quite rich. While I love that style of preparation, I wanted to create a different kind of sweet potato recipe: still sweet, but light and airy and full of spices and vanilla. And of course I wanted to start with canned sweet potatoes for their convenience. A soufflé might sound intimidating, but my hope is that this recipe normalizes making soufflés on a regular basis. After making this version, you'll no longer fear your soufflé deflating and will feel confident adding it to your repertoire of impressive dishes. I serve this with Air-Fried Chicken Tenders (page 73) or Instant Pot Barbecue Ribs (page 132).*

| | |
|---|---|
| 1 | (15-ounce) can sweet potato puree |
| ¾ | cup plus 2 tablespoons sweetened condensed milk |
| ¼ | cup maple syrup |
| ¼ | cup heavy cream |
| 2 | large eggs, separated, plus 1 large white |
| ½ | teaspoon vanilla bean paste |
| ¼ | teaspoon ground nutmeg |
| ¼ | teaspoon ground cinnamon |
| ¼ | teaspoon ground ginger |
| ¼ | teaspoon cream of tartar |

**1**  Adjust oven rack to middle position and heat oven to 375 degrees. Grease 8-inch square baking dish or pan. Whisk sweet potato puree, condensed milk, maple syrup, heavy cream, egg yolks, vanilla bean paste, nutmeg, cinnamon, and ginger in large bowl until well combined; set aside.

**2**  Using stand mixer fitted with whisk attachment, whip egg whites and cream of tartar on medium-low speed until foamy, about 1 minute. Increase speed to medium-high and whip until stiff peaks form, 3 to 4 minutes.

**3**  Transfer one-third of whipped egg whites to sweet potato mixture and whisk gently until mixture is lightened. Using rubber spatula, gently fold remaining egg whites into sweet potato mixture. Pour batter into prepared dish and smooth top with rubber spatula.

**4**  Bake until top is set and edges are golden brown, 30 to 35 minutes. Serve immediately.

## Antoinette's Tip

Gently folding in a portion of the beaten egg whites with a rubber spatula keeps some of the egg foam intact, making for a lighter, taller soufflé. Even so, it will start to deflate rather quickly after it comes out of the oven. It will still taste delicious, but for maximum visual appeal, serve it right away!

## Antoinette's Tip

For maximum scoopability, let this ice cream sit on the counter to soften for about 10 minutes before serving.

# No-Churn Sweet Potato Pie Ice Cream

**Serves:** 8 to 10 (makes 1 quart)  ·  **Total time:** 15 minutes, plus 6 hours freezing

*In episode nine of America's Test Kitchen: The Next Generation, we had three hours to create a three-course meal for the judges that showed them a bit of who we were and where we came from. For my dessert, I wanted to highlight family traditions of eating my granny's sweet potato pie and going to our favorite ice cream shop on summer nights, so I came up with a sweet potato pie ice cream. That was the first time I had ever made ice cream, and it was a little nerve-racking. But the result wowed the judges and made me realize that hey, maybe I can make desserts. If Jack Bishzop says it's his favorite, I must be doing something right! To make this failproof for everyone at home, I simplified my ingredients and borrowed a tried-and-true no-churn technique developed by Morgan Bolling, executive editor of Cook's Country. Enjoy this on its own or top it with crushed graham crackers and whipped cream.*

| | |
|---|---|
| 2 | cups heavy cream, chilled |
| 1 | cup sweetened condensed milk |
| 1 | cup canned sweet potato puree |
| ¼ | cup whole milk |
| ¼ | cup light corn syrup |
| 2 | tablespoons sugar |
| 1 | teaspoon vanilla bean paste |
| ½ | teaspoon ground ginger |
| ½ | teaspoon ground cinnamon |
| ½ | teaspoon ground nutmeg |
| ¼ | teaspoon table salt |

**1** Process cream in blender until soft peaks form, 20 to 30 seconds. Scrape down sides of blender jar and continue to process until stiff peaks form, about 10 seconds longer. Using rubber spatula, stir in condensed milk, sweet potato puree, milk, corn syrup, sugar, vanilla bean paste, ginger, cinnamon, nutmeg, and salt. Process until thoroughly combined, about 20 seconds, scraping down sides of blender jar as needed.

**2** Pour cream mixture into 8½ by 4½-inch loaf pan. Press plastic wrap flush against surface of cream mixture. Freeze until firm, at least 6 hours. Serve.

## *Pantry Pick*

**Sweetened condensed milk:** This dessert hero ingredient is made by heating milk to remove a lot of its water and then adding sugar. It's key to creating this ice cream's smooth, thick texture. Look for a brand that contains only milk and sugar; the test kitchen's favorites are Borden Eagle Brand Sweetened Condensed Milk and Nestlé Carnation Sweetened Condensed Milk.

# Cherry-Bourbon Trifle

**Serves:** 8 to 10   ·   **Total time:** 25 minutes, plus 6 hours chilling

*Want to know my go-to party dish? It's this fruity, creamy, cakey trifle. It's simple to make, it looks impressive, and it's so, so good. I start with a foundation of store-bought pound cake, soaked in bourbon. Then I build layers with the cake, sweet canned cherries, and vanilla-maple whipped cream to create a dessert that definitely does not lack in flavor. You may be wondering what the cream cheese is doing here. I always add it when I make whipped cream, because it not only adds flavor but also stops the whipped cream from deflating. Don't be afraid to experiment with switching up the flavors. I've used lemon-flavored cake and canned blueberry pie filling—the possibilities are endless! I like to use a 2-quart trifle dish for this recipe; however, you can also use a 2-quart bowl. You could also build and serve individual trifles in eight 1-cup jars or cups. Garnish with Candied Walnuts (page 184), if you like.*

¼   cup bourbon

1   pound store-bought pound cake, cut into 1-inch squares

2   tablespoons cream cheese

1   cup heavy cream, divided

½   teaspoon vanilla bean paste

¾   cup maple syrup

1   (21-ounce) can whole cherry pie filling

**1**   Drizzle bourbon over cake pieces in bowl, tossing halfway through drizzling to ensure cake is evenly coated; set aside.

**2**   Microwave cream cheese in medium bowl until very soft, about 20 seconds. Add ¼ cup cream and whisk vigorously until smooth, then transfer to bowl of stand mixer. Add remaining cream and vanilla bean paste and whip using whisk attachment on medium-low speed until well combined and foamy, about 1 minute. Add maple syrup, increase speed to medium-high, and beat until stiff peaks form, 1 to 3 minutes.

**3**   Arrange one-third of reserved bourbon-soaked cake pieces in even layer in bottom of 2-quart trifle dish. Top with one-third of cherries and one-third of maple whipped cream. Repeat layering with remaining cake, cherries, and maple whipped cream. Cover with plastic wrap and refrigerate for at least 6 hours or up to 24 hours. Serve.

## *Pantry Pick*

**Vanilla bean paste:** This dark, thick paste is an easy one-to-one swap with vanilla extract, and I often prefer it because it has a more intense flavor than extract and gets you those pretty flecks that will make it seem like you used whole vanilla beans. The test kitchen's favorite is Nielsen-Massey Pure Vanilla Bean Paste.

### Antoinette's Tip

Typically when you make whipped cream, you would start with chilled ingredients, because cold cream whips faster and higher. But microwaving the cream cheese to soften it is the best way to ensure that it's fully incorporated with the heavy cream. Don't worry that the mixture isn't totally chilled—it will still whip up just fine.

# Chapter 2

## Make the Most of Pantry Ingredients

Hot Honey Mustard Slaw
with Peanuts

Chopped Salad with Creamy
Garlic Dressing

Spicy Potato Salad with
Honey-Chipotle Dressing

Barbecue Sauce

Barbecue Spice Rub

Brown Sugar–Soy Sauce Stir-Fry

Shrimp Caesar Wrap

Air-Fried Cod with Fried Food Sauce

Mustard Fried Branzino

The Perfect Steak

Lamb Meatballs in Gravy

Pork Chops, Stuffing, and Gravy

Creamy Dijon-Rosemary Chicken

Air-Fried Chicken Tenders with
Chipotle Mayo

Curry-Braised Chicken Leg Quarters

Hot Pepper–Strawberry Wings

Air-Fried Game Day Wings

# Hot Honey Mustard Slaw with Peanuts

**Serves:** 6 to 8  ·  **Total time:** 10 minutes

*This crunchy slaw comes together in just a few minutes with a base of bagged shredded green cabbage and sugar snap peas. At the heart of this extraordinary (and extraordinarily simple) side dish is the dressing, which features a dynamic, if unexpected, duo of hot Chinese mustard and peanut butter. The hot mustard adds a kick of clean heat, while the peanut butter lends a rich and nutty undertone. A splash of soy sauce gives the dressing an irresistible salty-savory note, and the honey mellows out all of those intense flavors. Sprinkling chopped peanuts and crispy wonton strips over the slaw before serving adds to the crunchy delight. You'll have left-over dressing, which you can effortlessly pair with other premade slaw mixes. I especially like the bagged blend featuring cabbage and broccoli. You could also thin leftover dressing with a little water and toss it with cooked noodles.*

1  (14-ounce) bag green coleslaw mix

6  ounces sugar snap peas, strings removed, sliced ¼ inch thick on bias

½  cup Hot Honey Mustard–Peanut Dressing

1  cup wonton strips

3  tablespoons chopped dry-roasted peanuts

Combine coleslaw mix, snap peas, and dressing in bowl and toss to coat. Sprinkle with wonton strips and peanuts and serve.

## Hot Honey Mustard–Peanut Dressing

**Makes:** 1 cup  ·  **Total time:** 5 minutes

6  tablespoons Chinese hot mustard

¼  cup honey

¼  cup soy sauce

2  tablespoons peanut butter

Whisk all ingredients together in bowl. (Dressing can be refrigerated in airtight container for up to 1 week.)

## *Pantry Pick*

**Chinese hot mustard:** You might find packets of this in your Chinese takeout bag when you order egg rolls or spring rolls. It has a sharp pungency that's reminiscent of horseradish or wasabi. If you can't find Chinese hot mustard at your supermarket, look for Colman's English Mustard, which is a good substitute.

# Chopped Salad with Creamy Garlic Dressing

**Serves:** 4 · **Total time:** 10 minutes

*This simple, fresh chopped salad is just as satisfying packed for lunch as it is served for a light dinner or alongside some simple grilled chicken. One of the best parts of this recipe is the homemade garlic dressing, which is creamy and rich from mayo and Pecorino Romano, tangy from vinegar, and packed with two forms of pantry-friendly garlic for double the punch. Making your own dressing is not only incredibly easy but also gives you complete control over the ingredients and quantities. With a dressing recipe this fresh and flavorful, you'll never need to buy a bottle of overpriced dressing at the supermarket again.*

1 (15-ounce) can chickpeas, rinsed

1 romaine lettuce heart (6 ounces), cut into ½-inch pieces

½ cup pitted kalamata olives, chopped

½ small red onion, chopped fine

1 carrot, peeled and shredded

1 celery rib, sliced ¼ inch thick

½ cup Creamy Garlic Dressing

Toss all ingredients in large bowl until evenly coated with dressing. Season with salt and pepper to taste. Serve.

## Creamy Garlic Dressing

**Makes:** 1 cup · **Total time:** 10 minutes

½ cup mayonnaise

⅓ cup extra-virgin olive oil

¼ cup white wine vinegar

¼ cup grated Pecorino Romano cheese

2 garlic cloves, minced

½ teaspoon Italian seasoning

½ teaspoon garlic powder

Whisk all ingredients together in large bowl or container. (Dressing can be refrigerated in airtight container for up to 1 week.)

## *Pantry Pick*

**Garlic powder:** Time-saving and longer-lasting than fresh garlic, garlic powder is more than just a shortcut or an alternative to fresh garlic. When it's the only garlic in a recipe, it adds warmth without the punch of fresh garlic. When used along with fresh cloves, as in this dressing, garlic powder brings an extra layer of complexity.

# Spicy Potato Salad with Honey-Chipotle Dressing

**Serves:** 6 to 8 · **Total time:** 30 minutes, plus 30 minutes cooling

*If you're like me and find the various mayo-heavy versions of traditional potato salad overwhelming, fear not, for I have crafted a pantry-friendly recipe that is bursting with spicy, sweet, and tangy flavors. The smoky allure at the heart of this dish comes from chipotle chiles in adobo sauce. These fiery gems bring a captivatingly rich depth to every bite. Blended with honey, wine vinegar, and olive oil, they create a bold dressing that coats the potatoes with just the right balance of sweet and heat. Their smokiness is boosted a bit more by adding bacon to the salad. You'll have dressing left over, which is delicious on salads with avocados or black beans, brushed onto corn on the cob, or drizzled over chicken or steak.*

3 pounds red potatoes, peeled and cut into ¾-inch pieces

¼ teaspoon table salt, plus salt for cooking potatoes

8 slices fully cooked bacon, chopped

½ cup Honey-Chipotle Dressing

4 scallions, sliced thin

**1** Bring potatoes, 1 tablespoon salt, and enough water to cover by 1 inch to boil in large pot over high heat. Reduce heat to medium and simmer until potatoes are tender, 10 to 15 minutes.

**2** Drain potatoes, then spread in even layer on rimmed baking sheet; refrigerate until cooled, about 30 minutes.

**3** Combine cooled potatoes in large bowl with bacon, dressing, scallions, and salt and toss to combine. Serve.

## Honey-Chipotle Dressing

**Makes:** 1¾ cups · **Total time:** 5 minutes

1 (7-ounce) can chipotle chiles in adobo sauce

¼ cup honey

2 tablespoons red wine vinegar

¼ teaspoon table salt

⅔ cup extra-virgin olive oil

Process chipotles, honey, vinegar, and salt in blender until smooth, 15 to 30 seconds, scraping down sides of blender jar as needed. With blender running, slowly add oil until incorporated. (Dressing can be refrigerated in airtight container for up to 1 week.)

## *Pantry Pick*

**Chipotle chiles in adobo:** These smoked jalapeños in a tomato- and vinegar-based adobo sauce deliver strong, smoky heat. You use the whole can for this dressing, but when you do have leftovers, you can freeze them in tablespoon-size dollops on a plate and then transfer them to a freezer storage container.

# Barbecue Sauce

**Makes:** 1½ cups · **Total time:** 10 minutes

*This robust Kansas City–inspired sauce embraces the sweeter, smokier side of barbecue. The ketchup lays a sweet-tangy base. Molasses and bourbon add deep sweetness, while liquid smoke imparts that essential smoky essence. One of the joys of this sauce is how it effortlessly pairs with my Barbecue Spice Rub, creating a truly dynamic duo.*

| | |
|---|---|
| 1 | cup ketchup |
| ½ | cup packed dark brown sugar |
| ¼ | cup molasses |
| 3 | tablespoons bourbon |
| ⅛ | teaspoon liquid smoke |

Combine all ingredients in medium saucepan. Bring to boil over medium-high heat, then reduce heat to medium-low and simmer until sugar has dissolved and sauce has thickened slightly, about 3 minutes. Let cool, then store in airtight container in refrigerator for up to 1 week.

## *Pantry Pick*

**Ketchup:** I actually don't use ketchup all that often in my kitchen. As you'll see throughout this book, I'm much more of a mustard fan when it comes to adding bold flavor through condiments. However, for a Kansas City–style barbecue sauce, it's a must. The test kitchen likes Heinz Organic Tomato Ketchup.

# Barbecue Spice Rub

**Makes:** ¾ cup  ·  **Total time:** 10 minutes

*An artful infusion of heat sets this rub apart. Calibrated amounts of savory spices create a complex, invigorating warmth. I like things on the spicy side, but you can adjust the cayenne for less fire. Then, to achieve the ideal spicy-sweet balance that I find essential in a barbecue rub, I've included dark brown sugar. Its molasses-like sweetness provides sublime contrast to the spices and promotes a caramelized crust on meats.*

| | |
|---|---|
| ¼ | cup packed dark brown sugar |
| 1–2 | tablespoons cayenne pepper |
| 1 | tablespoon garlic powder |
| 1 | tablespoon onion powder |
| 1 | tablespoon smoked paprika |
| 1 | tablespoon chili powder |
| 1 | tablespoon dry mustard |
| 1 | tablespoon dried oregano |
| 1 | teaspoon ground cumin |

Combine all ingredients in bowl. Store in airtight container for up to 1 month.

## *Pantry Pick*

**Onion powder:** Made from dehydrated ground onion, this can include any variety of onion and may or may not include the skins, stems, or roots. For a strong oniony punch, you can use it just like you'd use garlic powder. Also like garlic powder, you can use onion powder alone or in conjunction with fresh onion for a more layered flavor.

## Antoinette's Tips

You can use a 1-pound frozen stir-fry vegetable blend, thawed, in place of the stir-fry kits, if you like.

Serve this as a side dish or make a light meal by spooning it over rice.

# Brown Sugar–Soy Sauce Stir-Fry

**Serves:** 4   ·   **Total time:** 20 minutes

*With just a few simple ingredients, this irresistible glaze transforms plain sliced vegetables into a sensational culinary experience. The sauces that come with refrigerated stir-fry meal kits are typically loaded with sodium and other questionable ingredients, so making your own is always better in terms of quality and flavor. The magic here begins by whisking together water and cornstarch, creating a smooth mixture that will help thicken the glaze. Then, the remaining ingredients join the party, whisked until the brown sugar dissolves, resulting in a luscious, velvety glaze that's extremely versatile. It's the perfect opportunity to breathe fresh life into practically any vegetable.*

6   tablespoons water, divided

2   tablespoons cornstarch

⅓   cup soy sauce

¼   cup packed dark brown sugar

2   tablespoons seasoned rice vinegar

1   tablespoon toasted sesame oil

3   garlic cloves, minced

1   teaspoon ground ginger

¼   teaspoon red pepper flakes

1   tablespoon vegetable oil

2   (12.5-ounce) bags stir-fry vegetable kit, sauce packets discarded

**1**   Whisk ¼ cup water and cornstarch in medium bowl until combined. Add soy sauce, sugar, vinegar, sesame oil, garlic, ginger, and pepper flakes and whisk until sugar is dissolved. Set aside.

**2**   Heat vegetable oil in 12-inch nonstick skillet over medium heat until shimmering. Add vegetables and cook for 30 seconds. Stir in remaining 2 tablespoons water, then cover skillet and cook until vegetables are crisp-tender, 2 to 4 minutes.

**3**   Whisk reserved sauce to recombine, then add to skillet. Cook, stirring frequently, until sauce is thickened slightly, about 1 minute. Serve.

## *Pantry Pick*

**Dark brown sugar:** In recipes both sweet and savory, I reach for dark brown sugar because its higher molasses content adds a more complex, toffee-like flavor. You can substitute light brown sugar in any recipe if that's what you have in your pantry.

# Shrimp Caesar Wrap

**Serves:** 4 (makes 4 wraps)  ·  **Total time:** 35 minutes

*Wraps, oh wraps, how they have convinced us (or at least me) that anything enveloped in a tortilla instantly becomes healthy! It's like the magical powers of the tortilla transform our lunch into a nutritional wonderland. But hey, who are we to argue with the mystical ways of the wrap? In all seriousness, though, stashing flour tortillas and shrimp in your freezer gives you a fantastic option for a quick and easy lunch that doesn't compromise on taste. For my homemade Caesar dressing, I ensure a perfect emulsification every time by using a blender. This simple technique lets me blend together elements that don't easily combine—oil and acid—to create a luscious dressing that clings perfectly to every morsel of the salad.*

1½  pounds extra-large shrimp (21 to 25 per pound), peeled, deveined, and tails removed

1  tablespoon extra-virgin olive oil

1  cup Caesar Dressing, divided

1  head romaine lettuce heart (6 ounces), chopped

½  English cucumber, quartered lengthwise and sliced ¼ inch thick

4  (12-inch) flour tortillas

**1**  Pat shrimp dry with paper towels. Heat oil in 12-inch nonstick skillet over medium heat until shimmering. Add half of shrimp to skillet in single layer and cook until spotty brown and edges begin to turn pink, about 1 minute. Off heat, flip shrimp, cover, and cook second side using residual heat of skillet until shrimp are opaque throughout, 1 to 2 minutes. Transfer shrimp to plate; repeat with remaining shrimp. Let shrimp cool for 5 minutes.

**2**  Toss shrimp with ¼ cup dressing in bowl. Toss lettuce and cucumbers with remaining ¾ cup dressing in second bowl. Distribute shrimp and lettuce mixture evenly on bottom third of each tortilla. Working with 1 wrap at a time, fold sides of tortilla over filling, fold bottom of tortilla over sides and filling, and roll tightly. Serve.

## Caesar Dressing

**Makes:** 1 cup  ·  **Total time:** 10 minutes

3  tablespoons lemon juice

2  tablespoons Dijon mustard

3  garlic cloves, minced

1  large egg yolk

5  anchovy fillets, rinsed, patted dry, and minced

½  cup extra-virgin olive oil

1  ounce Parmesan cheese, grated (½ cup)

½  teaspoon pepper

¼  teaspoon table salt

Process lemon juice, Dijon, garlic, egg yolk, and anchovies in blender until smooth, about 30 seconds. With blender running, slowly add oil until incorporated. Transfer dressing to large bowl and whisk in Parmesan, pepper, and salt. (Dressing can be refrigerated in airtight container for up to 3 days.)

# Air-Fried Cod with Fried Food Sauce

**Serves:** 2 · **Total time:** 35 minutes

*If you love fish and chips but are looking for a quicker, healthier (and pantry-friendly) twist on the fried fish, here's your recipe. The air fryer lets you enjoy crispy, flaky fried white fish without the hassle of maneuvering a heavy Dutch oven and large quantities of hot oil. In this recipe, I'm taking a lighter approach to that classic stovetop fried fish by utilizing the air fryer's power of hot air circulation to achieve an irresistible crunchy crust. I first dredge the fillets in seasoned flour and then in hot sauce–spiked beaten egg. This lays a solid foundation for dredging the fillets in the flaky panko bread crumbs (which are also seasoned). The result is an even, golden-brown coating. The fried food sauce is my Southern-style update on tartar sauce, and once you taste it, I promise you'll be dunking everything into it! I also love it with Air-Fried Chicken Tenders (page 73) and Air-Fried Game Day Wings (page 78).*

½ cup panko bread crumbs

1 teaspoon garlic powder, divided

1 teaspoon onion powder, divided

1 teaspoon paprika, divided

¼ cup all-purpose flour

1 large egg

1 tablespoon hot sauce

2 (6- to 8-ounce) skinless cod fillets, 1 to 1½ inches thick

½ teaspoon table salt

¼ cup Fried Food Sauce

**1** Make sling for air-fryer basket by folding 1 long sheet of aluminum foil so it is 4 inches wide. Lay sheet of foil width wide across basket, pressing foil into and up sides of basket. Fold excess foil as needed so edges of foil are flush with top of basket. Lightly spray foil with vegetable oil spray.

**2** Combine panko, ½ teaspoon garlic powder, ½ teaspoon onion powder, and ½ teaspoon paprika in shallow dish. Combine flour, remaining ½ teaspoon garlic powder, remaining ½ teaspoon onion powder, and remaining ½ teaspoon paprika in second shallow dish. Lightly beat egg and hot sauce in third shallow dish.

**3** Pat cod dry with paper towels and sprinkle evenly with salt. Working with 1 fillet at a time, dredge in flour, shaking off excess; dip in egg mixture, allowing excess to drip off; and coat with panko mixture, pressing gently to adhere.

**4** Arrange fillets on prepared sling, spaced evenly apart, and lightly spray all over with vegetable oil spray. Place basket in air fryer and set temperature to 400 degrees. Cook until panko is golden and cod flakes apart when gently prodded with paring knife and registers 135 degrees, 10 to 15 minutes, flipping halfway through.

**5** Using sling, carefully remove cod from air fryer. Transfer to individual plates or platter and serve with sauce.

## *Pantry Pick*

### Worcestershire sauce:

This umami powerhouse is used in countless marinades and sauces and has become an essential ingredient in the Bloody Mary. Its base is vinegar, to which a variety of seasonings including molasses, tamarind, onion, garlic, and anchovies are added. The test kitchen's favorite is Lea & Perrins Original Worcestershire Sauce.

### Fried Food Sauce

**Makes:** ¾ cup
**Total time:** 10 minutes

½   cup mayonnaise

¼   cup ketchup

2   teaspoons Worcestershire sauce

1   teaspoon hot sauce

1   teaspoon garlic powder

1   teaspoon table salt

1   teaspoon Cajun seasoning

½   teaspoon smoked paprika

Whisk all ingredients together in bowl. (Sauce can be refrigerated for up to 1 week.)

# Mustard Fried Branzino

**Serves:** 2 to 4  ·  **Total time:** 45 minutes

*Here's my twist on the classic Southern dish of mustard fried catfish. With its origins deeply rooted in Southern cuisine, this branzino pays homage to the beloved tradition while introducing a tantalizing, pantry-friendly flavor update. Branzino is a Mediterranean fish known for its delicate flavor and tender, flaky flesh. Branzino shares some similarities with catfish, such as its firm texture and its ability to hold up well to frying (in this case, shallow frying). However, branzino brings its own unique qualities to this preparation. Its milder flavor allows the flavors of the mustard and other seasonings to shine strong. Brushing the spice-rubbed fish with yellow mustard not only adds tangy flavor but also helps the flour adhere to form a crust, sealing in the natural juices of the fish during the frying process. This ensures that each bite remains moist and succulent.*

2    teaspoons kosher salt

2    teaspoons garlic powder

1    teaspoon pepper

½    teaspoon paprika

1    cup all-purpose flour

2    (1- to 1½-pound) whole branzino, scaled, gutted, fins snipped off with scissors

2    tablespoons yellow mustard

1    quart vegetable oil, for frying

    Hot sauce

    Lemon wedges

## *Pantry Pick*

**Yellow mustard:** Pungent and acidic without a lot of added spices, yellow mustard is a super versatile way to add zingy flavor to a lot more than just ballpark hot dogs. The test kitchen likes Heinz Yellow Mustard.

**1**    Adjust oven rack to middle position and heat oven to 200 degrees. Combine salt, garlic powder, pepper, and paprika in small bowl. Place flour in shallow dish, add 2 teaspoons salt-spice mixture, and whisk to combine.

**2**    Rinse each branzino under cold running water and pat dry with paper towels inside and out. Using sharp knife, cut each branzino in half crosswise, then make three ½-inch-deep slashes about 1 inch apart on both sides of each piece of branzino. Sprinkle remaining salt-spice mixture evenly over both exterior and interior cavity of each piece of branzino, then brush both sides with mustard. Working with 1 piece at a time, coat both sides lightly with flour mixture, shaking off excess, and place on wire rack set in rimmed baking sheet.

**3**    Set wire rack in second rimmed baking sheet. Add oil to Dutch oven until it measures about 1 inch deep and heat over medium-high heat until it registers 350 degrees. Add 2 pieces branzino to hot oil and fry until golden brown, crisp, and registers 140 degrees, 3 to 5 minutes on each side. Adjust burner, if necessary, to maintain oil temperature between 350 and 375 degrees. Using 2 spatulas, carefully remove branzino from oil and place on prepared rack to drain. Transfer sheet to oven to keep warm, return oil to 350 degrees, and repeat with remaining branzino. Serve, passing hot sauce and lemon wedges separately.

### Antoinette's Tip

If your market doesn't have whole branzino, try whole black sea bass or red snapper instead.

# The Perfect Steak

**Serves:** 2   ·   **Total time:** 25 minutes, plus 45 minutes resting

*Naming something "perfect" might raise eyebrows, but trust me, with the right techniques and proper attention to detail, you can create a stovetop steak culinary experience that will surpass your wildest expectations. First, allowing your steak to sit at room temperature for 45 minutes helps it cook more evenly. Second, patting it dry before cooking helps the exterior brown more evenly. Third, flipping the steak frequently as it cooks maximizes moisture evaporation, allowing a crisper crust to form while also promoting uniform cooking. The type of pan also plays a significant role. A heavy skillet that retains heat well, preferably cast iron, is an excellent choice. Remember to preheat the pan properly to achieve that perfect sear. Now, let's talk about my All-Purpose Seasoning. I designed it to complement a variety of foods, making it a go-to pantry option (check out the Pork Chops, Stuffing, and Gravy on page 69 and the Creamy Dijon-Rosemary Chicken on page 70 for more ways to use it). This seasoning doesn't include salt, so you can season to taste. Flake sea salt would be perfect here.*

1   (1-pound) boneless strip steak, 1½ inches thick, trimmed

½   teaspoon table salt

1   tablespoon vegetable oil

1   tablespoon All-Purpose Seasoning

**1**   Cut steak in half crosswise to create two 8-ounce steaks. Pat steaks dry with paper towels, then sprinkle all over with salt. Let sit for 45 minutes.

**2**   Pat steaks dry with paper towels, then sprinkle all over with all-purpose seasoning. Heat oil in 10-inch skillet over medium-high heat until just smoking. Place steaks in skillet and cook without moving for 30 seconds. Flip steaks and continue to cook for 30 seconds. Continue flipping steaks every 30 seconds until steak registers 130 to 135 degrees (for medium), about 8 minutes.

**3**   Transfer steak to cutting board, tent with aluminum foil, and let rest for 5 minutes. Serve.

---

## All-Purpose Seasoning

**Makes:** ¼ cup

Total time: 5 minutes

2   tablespoons garlic powder

2   tablespoons onion powder

½   teaspoon cayenne pepper

½   teaspoon mustard powder

½   teaspoon dried oregano

Combine all ingredients in bowl. (Seasoning mix can be stored in airtight container at room temperature for up to 1 month.)

# Lamb Meatballs in Gravy

**Serves:** 4 · **Total time:** 50 minutes

*If you haven't cooked lamb before, fear not! Here's a sensational introductory recipe. When working with strongly flavored meats like lamb, it's essential to embrace their distinctiveness. Here I turn ground lamb into easy meatballs by blending the meat with Greek yogurt, panko bread crumbs, and egg. Plenty of bold herbs and spices enhance the flavor of the lamb. I brown the meatballs all over in a skillet first, then set them aside to build a robust pan gravy with shallot, beef broth, and red wine. Allspice adds a hint of warmth to the sauce. The juicy tenderness of the meatballs is best preserved when they are cooked to a medium doneness, so be mindful not to overcook them. Also take care to brown the meatballs thoroughly in step 2, as this adds an appetizing golden crust that enhances both texture and flavor. You can serve these as is, but I like to serve them over rice to soak up every drop of the gravy.*

¼ cup panko bread crumbs

¼ cup plain Greek yogurt

1 large egg

1½ teaspoons dried dill, plus extra for serving

1 teaspoon garlic powder

¾ teaspoon table salt, divided

¾ teaspoon dried oregano

½ teaspoon ground cumin

¼ teaspoon pepper

1 pound ground lamb

1 tablespoon extra-virgin olive oil

1 shallot, minced

1 tablespoon all-purpose flour

¼ teaspoon ground allspice

1 cup beef broth

1 cup water

¼ cup red wine

**1** Combine panko, yogurt, egg, dill, garlic powder, ½ teaspoon salt, oregano, cumin, and pepper in large bowl, stirring well. Add lamb and mix with your hands until thoroughly combined. Roll into sixteen 1½-inch meatballs (about 2 tablespoons each) between your wet hands; transfer to plate.

**2** Heat oil in 12-inch nonstick skillet over medium heat until shimmering. Add meatballs and cook until browned all over, about 10 minutes. Transfer meatballs to clean plate, reserving fat in skillet, and set aside.

**3** Add shallot to fat left in skillet and cook over medium heat until softened, about 3 minutes. Add flour and allspice and cook, stirring constantly, for 1 minute. Whisk in broth, water, wine, and remaining ¼ teaspoon salt, scraping up any browned bits. Cook until gravy is thickened slightly, 3 to 5 minutes.

**4** Return meatballs and any accumulated juices to skillet and cook until meatballs register 160 degrees, about 5 minutes. Sprinkle meatballs with extra dill and serve.

# Pork Chops, Stuffing, and Gravy

**Serves:** 4   ·   **Total time:** 1 hour, plus 30 minutes brining

*Most families have some version of pork chops and stuffing in their physical or virtual recipe box, and mine is no different. This recipe pays homage to the beloved "Aunt Edna's pork chops" that my mom used to make, inspired by the convenience of store-bought stuffing mix. Here I've taken Aunt Edna's recipe up a notch. In the original, cream of mushroom soup played a big role, but I've left that out in favor of vegetables, garlic, and my All-Purpose Seasoning. A quick brine adds moisture to the chops. Nestling the browned chops right in the stuffing mixture to bake both infuses the stuffing with delicious meaty juices and also helps keep the chops juicy as they finish in the oven.*

⅓  cup table salt for brining

⅓  cup packed brown sugar for brining

4  (6- to 8-ounce) boneless pork chops, 1-inch-thick, trimmed

2  tablespoons extra-virgin olive oil, divided

1  carrot, peeled and cut into ¼-inch pieces

1  celery rib, chopped fine

2  shallots, minced, divided

1  teaspoon All-Purpose Seasoning (page 65), divided

8  tablespoons unsalted butter, divided

4  cups chicken broth, divided

1  (6-ounce) package stuffing mix

¼  cup all-purpose flour

4  garlic cloves, minced

¼  teaspoon table salt

**1**  Adjust oven rack to middle position and heat oven to 400 degrees. Dissolve salt and sugar in 1½ quarts cold water in large container. Add chops, cover, and refrigerate for 30 minutes to 1 hour.

**2**  Meanwhile, heat 1 tablespoon oil in 12-inch skillet over medium heat until shimmering. Add carrot, celery, half of shallot, and ½ teaspoon all-purpose seasoning and cook until carrots are softened, about 10 minutes. Add 4 tablespoons butter and stir until melted. Transfer vegetables to 13 by 9-inch baking dish. Add 1½ cups broth and stuffing mix to vegetables, stirring to combine. Wipe out skillet.

**3**  Remove chops from brine and pat dry with paper towels. Heat remaining 1 tablespoon oil in now-empty skillet over medium-high heat until just smoking. Add chops and cook until well browned on 1 side, 3 to 5 minutes. Remove skillet from heat. Nestle chops, browned side up, into reserved stuffing mixture in dish. Transfer to oven and roast until chops register 140 degrees, 10 to 12 minutes.

**4**  Meanwhile, melt remaining 4 tablespoons butter in again-empty skillet over medium heat. Add remaining shallot and cook until softened, about 3 minutes. Add flour, garlic, salt, and remaining ½ teaspoon all-purpose seasoning and cook, stirring constantly, for 1 minute. Whisk in ½ cup water and remaining 2½ cups broth and bring to simmer over medium-high heat. Reduce heat to medium-low and simmer until thickened slightly, 7 to 10 minutes. Transfer gravy to serving dish and serve with chops and stuffing.

# Creamy Dijon-Rosemary Chicken

**Serves:** 4  ·  **Total time:** 35 minutes

*This quick skillet meal is perfect for a weeknight dinner when you're craving something satisfying yet easy to pull together. For this recipe, I harness the power of two key pantry ingredients: dried rosemary and Dijon mustard. The fragrant rosemary adds an earthy, piney note to the dish. The Dijon mustard adds a bit of warm spice, and combining it with cream and chicken broth to make the pan sauce mellows it out. For the chicken, I start by seasoning the boneless breasts with my trusty All-Purpose Seasoning, ensuring that every bite is flavorful. I brown the lean chicken in oil and butter for extra richness and then set it aside to sauté onion and garlic and build the pan sauce. The addition of flour helps to thicken the sauce, creating a velvety texture. I like to serve this alongside simple roasted potatoes or steamed vegetables.*

2    (6- to 8-ounce) boneless skinless chicken breasts, trimmed

1    tablespoon All-Purpose Seasoning (page 65)

½    teaspoon table salt

2    tablespoons extra-virgin olive oil, divided

1    tablespoon unsalted butter

1    onion, sliced thin

3    garlic cloves, minced

¼    teaspoon dried rosemary

1    tablespoon all-purpose flour

1    cup chicken broth

½    cup heavy cream

¼    cup Dijon mustard

    Lemon wedges

**1**    Working with 1 chicken breast at a time, starting on thick side, cut chicken in half horizontally (you should have 2 thin but nearly identical-looking breasts). Pat chicken dry with paper towels and sprinkle all over with all-purpose seasoning and salt.

**2**    Heat 1 tablespoon oil and butter in 12-inch skillet over medium heat until butter is melted and oil is shimmering. Add chicken in single layer and cook until lightly browned, 3 to 5 minutes per side. Transfer to plate.

**3**    Add remaining 1 tablespoon oil to now-empty skillet and heat over medium heat until shimmering. Add onion and cook until softened, about 5 minutes. Add garlic and rosemary and cook until fragrant, about 30 seconds. Stir in flour and cook for 1 minute. Whisk in broth, cream, and Dijon and bring to simmer. Return reserved chicken and any accumulated juices to skillet and cook until chicken is cooked through and sauce is thickened slightly, 3 to 5 minutes. Serve with lemon wedges.

## *Antoinette's Tips*

The smokiness of my Barbecue Spice Rub plays really well with the Chipotle Mayo, but you can use your favorite store-bought barbecue seasoning, if you prefer.

For a smooth mayo, I use only the sauce, not the actual chiles, from the can of chipotles. But you do you!

# Air-Fried Chicken Tenders with Chipotle Mayo

**Serves:** 2 · **Total time:** 20 minutes

*Crispy fried chicken without excess oil? Yes, please. These chicken tenders are "fried" to perfection in a flash in an air fryer, resulting in a golden exterior and juicy, tender meat. Fried chicken isn't just about the texture, though—it's also about the flavor, and I bring loads of that to the mild chicken by coating the tenders in yellow mustard and then dredging them in panko bread crumbs. Both the mustard and the crumbs are seasoned with my signature Barbecue Spice Rub, which brings smoky, spicy, sweet flavors. The Chipotle Mayo I like to serve these with for dipping brings even more bold smokiness to the table. Any leftover mayo is great for spreading on sandwiches.*

½ cup panko bread crumbs

3 tablespoons Barbecue Spice Rub (page 55), divided

3 tablespoons yellow mustard

1 teaspoon table salt

1 pound chicken tenderloins, trimmed

¼ cup Chipotle Mayo

**1** Lightly spray air-fryer basket with vegetable oil spray. Combine panko and 2 tablespoons barbecue seasoning in shallow dish. Whisk mustard, salt, and remaining 1 tablespoon barbecue seasoning together in large bowl. Pat chicken dry with paper towels, then add to bowl with mustard mixture and turn to coat.

**2** Working with 1 tenderloin at a time, coat in bread-crumb mixture, pressing lightly to adhere. Transfer to prepared air-fryer basket. Lightly spray chicken with vegetable oil spray. Place basket in air-fryer and set temperature to 400 degrees. Bake until chicken is golden brown and registers 160 degrees, 9 to 12 minutes, flipping halfway through cooking. Serve with chipotle mayo.

---

### Chipotle Mayo

**Makes:** ½ cup
**Total time:** 5 minutes

½ cup mayonnaise

1 tablespoon sauce from canned chipotle chiles in adobo sauce

1 tablespoon lime juice

⅛ teaspoon table salt

Combine mayonnaise, chipotle sauce, lime juice, and salt in bowl. (Sauce can be refrigerated for up to 1 week.)

# Curry-Braised Chicken Leg Quarters

**Serves:** 2 · **Total time:** 1 hour

*In this recipe, I unite the vibrant flavors of green curry paste and yellow curry powder. While these two ingredients originate from different culinary backgrounds, their combination adds layers of complexity to braised chicken leg quarters—one of my favorite cuts of chicken because of its economical price and ease of cooking. The Thai green curry paste infuses the chicken with its distinct flavors of green chile, garlic, ginger, and herbs, while the Indian-inspired curry powder enhances the spice profile with coriander, cumin, turmeric, more ginger, and other warm spices. I mash the seasonings together and rub them under the skin of the chicken; then I lightly brown the pieces in oil. Out comes the chicken and in goes onion, coconut milk, and chicken broth. The chicken goes back into the skillet to simmer gently, becoming ultratender as its collagen melts into the luxurious sauce.*

¼    cup Thai green curry paste, divided

1    teaspoon curry powder

1    teaspoon garlic powder

¼    teaspoon pepper

⅛    teaspoon plus ¼ teaspoon table salt, divided

2    (10- to 12-ounce) chicken leg quarters, trimmed

1    teaspoon vegetable oil

1    small onion, chopped fine

1    cup canned coconut milk

½    cup chicken broth

**1**    Using spatula, mash and stir 2 tablespoons curry paste, curry powder, garlic powder, pepper, and ⅛ teaspoon salt in bowl until combined. Using your fingers, gently loosen skin covering leg quarters and rub curry paste mixture directly on meat.

**2**    Heat oil in 10-inch nonstick skillet over medium heat until shimmering. Place chicken skin side down in skillet and cook until lightly browned on 1 side, 2 to 3 minutes; transfer chicken to plate. Add onion to fat left in skillet and cook until softened, about 3 minutes. Stir in remaining 2 tablespoons curry paste and cook until fragrant, about 1 minute.

**3**    Stir in coconut milk, broth, and remaining ¼ teaspoon salt, then add chicken, browned side up, and any accumulated juices. Bring to vigorous simmer over medium-high heat, then reduce heat to low. Cover and simmer gently until chicken registers at least 195 degrees, 30 to 40 minutes.

**4**    Transfer chicken to clean plate, tent with aluminum foil, and let rest for 5 minutes. Meanwhile, return sauce to simmer over medium heat and cook until thickened slightly, about 3 minutes, whisking occasionally. Serve chicken with sauce.

## Antoinette's Tips

I like to serve these chicken leg quarters over rice, noodles, or potatoes to soak up every bit of the flavorful sauce.

Use any leftover Thai green curry paste in the Coconut Green Curry Chicken Noodle Soup (page 87), or thin the paste with coconut milk and toss with noodles or rice.

### Antoinette's Tip

To make these wings faster, you can skip brining the wings in step 1. If you do, add an additional ¼ teaspoon salt to the garlic powder mixture in step 2.

# Hot Pepper–Strawberry Wings

**Serves:** 4 to 6   ·   **Total time:** 1½ hours, plus 30 minutes brining

*Strawberry preserves, a humble pantry staple, becomes the foundation for a tantalizingly sticky wing sauce that will have you licking your fingers—so serve these with plenty of napkins! Adding soy sauce, wine vinegar, and red pepper flakes to the preserves counterbalances their fruity sweetness, creating a bold, tangy sauce with a hint of heat. I brine the wings briefly to keep them nice and juicy through the two-step baking and broiling process, coating them with a spice mixture before baking them on a wire rack set in a baking sheet. Then I brush those babies generously with the sauce and pop them into the broiler for a few minutes to crisp and brown.*

| | |
|---|---|
| ½ | cup table salt for brining |
| 3 | pounds chicken wings, cut at joints, wing tips discarded |
| 1 | tablespoon garlic powder |
| 1½ | teaspoons onion powder |
| 1 | teaspoon smoked paprika |
| ½ | teaspoon sugar |
| ½ | teaspoon table salt |
| ½ | cup strawberry preserves |
| 1 | tablespoon soy sauce |
| 1 | tablespoon red wine vinegar |
| 1 | teaspoon red pepper flakes |

**1** Dissolve ½ cup salt in 2 quarts cold water in large container. Submerge chicken in brine, cover, and refrigerate for 30 minutes to 1 hour.

**2** Adjust oven rack 8 inches from broiler element and heat oven to 350 degrees. Line rimmed baking sheet with aluminum foil, then set wire rack in sheet and spray with vegetable oil spray. Combine garlic powder, onion powder, smoked paprika, sugar, and salt in bowl. Remove chicken from brine and pat dry with paper towels. Rub chicken all over with spice mixture.

**3** Arrange wings in single layer, fatty side up, on prepared rack. Bake until golden brown, about 1 hour.

**4** Combine strawberry preserves, soy sauce, vinegar, and pepper flakes in bowl. Remove wings from oven, and heat broiler. Brush exposed side of wings evenly with strawberry preserve mixture. Return wings to oven and broil until well browned, 3 to 5 minutes. Serve.

## *Pantry Pick*

**Strawberry preserves:** Of all the fruit spreads—jellies, jams, preserves—preserves have the fruitiest flavor, thanks to the larger chunks of fruit, so that's what I usually grab from the supermarket shelf. For another recipe that uses strawberry preserves, check out the Strawberry-Hoisin Meatballs (page 196). The test kitchen likes Smucker's Strawberry Preserves.

# Air-Fried Game Day Wings

**Serves:** 4 to 6   ·   **Total time:** 50 minutes, plus 30 minutes brining

*When I was growing up, Texas Pete hot sauce was a staple in my household, gracing our table during countless family gatherings and memorable game day feasts. Its distinct flavor has been a part of my culinary journey from the very beginning, and it evokes a sense of nostalgia and fond memories with every bite. Incorporating Texas Pete into these air-fried chicken wings not only adds incredible flavor but also pays homage to the cherished moments I shared with loved ones, making this recipe a true taste of home. To ensure the wings turn out tender and juicy, I brine them for 30 minutes. Then I pat them dry and coat them with a blend of garlic powder, onion powder, smoked paprika, and a touch of sweetness before air-frying. Blending the hot sauce with mustard and honey makes a tangy sauce for tossing the wings that will take your taste buds on a touchdown-worthy journey.*

½    cup table salt for brining

3    pounds chicken wings, cut at joints, wing tips discarded

2    tablespoons garlic powder

1    tablespoon onion powder

1    teaspoon smoked paprika

½    teaspoon sugar

½    teaspoon table salt

¾    cup Texas Pete hot sauce

2    tablespoons yellow mustard

2    teaspoons honey

**1**    Dissolve ½ cup salt in 2 quarts cold water in large container. Submerge chicken in brine, cover, and refrigerate for 30 minutes to 1 hour.

**2**    Combine garlic powder, onion powder, smoked paprika, sugar, and salt in bowl. Remove chicken from brine and pat dry with paper towels. Toss chicken in spice mixture. Arrange wings in air-fryer basket in single layer (they may overlap slightly). Place basket into air fryer and set temperature to 400 degrees. Cook until wings are golden brown, 35 to 40 minutes, flipping wings 3 times during cooking (about every 10 minutes).

**3**    Meanwhile, combine hot sauce, mustard, and honey in small saucepan. Cook over medium-high heat until reduced slightly, about 5 minutes. Toss wings with sauce in large bowl. Serve.

## Pantry Pick

**Louisiana-style hot sauce:** Distinguished from other types of hot sauce by its vinegar-forward flavor profile, Louisiana hot sauce brings a lot to the Southern table and to my recipes. Despite its name, Texas Pete Original Hot Sauce is a Louisiana-style sauce, and it's my hot sauce of choice. Tangy, pleasingly acidic, and just a touch sweet, Texas Pete has an irresistibly pure, straightforward heat.

### Antoinette's Tip

If you're in a hurry to get your game on, you can skip brining the wings in step 1. If you do, add an additional ¼ teaspoon salt to the garlic powder mixture in step 2.

# Chapter 3

## Reimagine Prepared Foods

Hoisin Chicken Lettuce Wraps

Barbecue Pulled Chicken Sandwiches

Coconut Green Curry Chicken
Noodle Soup

White Chicken Chili

Creamy Roasted Garlic and
Chicken Pasta

Mustard-Sesame Noodles

Chicken Enchilada Bake

Mini Chicken Pot Pies

Pesto Cheeseburgers

Air-Fried Pesto Chicken Roll-Ups

Air-Fried Pesto Salmon Fillet

Pesto-Stuffed Mushrooms

Herbed Goat Cheese Scramble

Butternut Squash and
Parmesan Soup

Chicken Gnocchi Soup

Air-Fried Crispy Gnocchi
with Artichokes

Crispy Gnocchi with Roasted
Red Pepper Sauce

Weeknight Ravioli Lasagna

Tortellini Salad

# Hoisin Chicken Lettuce Wraps

**Serves:** 4 to 6  ·  **Total time:** 25 minutes

*Rotisserie chicken, how versatile you are! With just a quick shred, this ready-to-eat supermarket staple is transformed into a superstar ingredient that effortlessly becomes the base for a wide variety of dishes. In these lettuce wraps, it takes center stage, providing a hearty and protein-rich filling that's enhanced with an explosion of flavors. Store-bought hoisin sauce pitches in to infuse the chicken with an irresistible blend of sweetness and umami. A dash of soy sauce and chili-garlic sauce add depth and a touch of heat, while grated fresh ginger wakes up everybody's taste buds. But it doesn't stop there—shredded carrots provide refreshing crunch and a burst of color, while roasted cashews bring satisfying texture and nutty undertones. This is truly a dish where convenience meets flavor.*

1 tablespoon extra-virgin olive oil

1 small onion, chopped fine

1 cup hoisin sauce

¼ cup water

2 tablespoons soy sauce

2 teaspoons chili-garlic sauce

1 teaspoon grated fresh ginger

1 (2½-pound) rotisserie chicken, skin and bones discarded, meat shredded into bite-size pieces (3 cups)

3 carrots, peeled and shredded

½ cup roasted cashews, chopped

2 tablespoons minced fresh cilantro

2 tablespoons lime juice, plus lime wedges for serving

1 head (8 ounces) Bibb lettuce or 1 small head (8 ounces) green leaf lettuce, leaves separated

**1** Heat oil in 12-inch nonstick skillet over medium heat until shimmering. Add onion and cook until softened, about 5 minutes. Stir in hoisin, water, soy sauce, chili-garlic sauce, and ginger and bring to simmer. Remove from heat and stir in chicken, carrots, cashews, cilantro, and lime juice.

**2** Serve chicken mixture in lettuce leaves with lime wedges.

## *Pantry Picks*

**Rotisserie chicken:** Store-bought rotisserie chicken is as delicious as it is convenient and is a genuine weeknight-dinner lifesaver. It pops up in several recipes in this chapter in various guises. For the most versatility in recipes, I buy plain rotisserie chickens.

**Hoisin sauce:** Fruity, tangy, and deeply savory, this thick, slightly grainy Chinese pantry staple is made from fermented soybeans, sugar, and various other ingredients depending on the brand. The test kitchen likes Kikkoman Hoisin Sauce.

# Barbecue Pulled Chicken Sandwiches

**Serves:** 4 · **Total time:** 20 minutes, plus 45 minutes resting

*As a true lover of Southern barbecue, I turn to this recipe when I yearn for that mouthwatering flavor but need a fast, convenient solution that doesn't involve firing up the grill or spending hours tending to slow-cooked meat. With the convenience of prepared rotisserie chicken and my trusty homemade barbecue sauce, these sandwiches are the epitome of easy and delicious dining. The pickled onions, a classic ATK recipe, are a cinch to make, and their chile spice and vinegary acidity counterbalance the sweetness of the saucy chicken.*

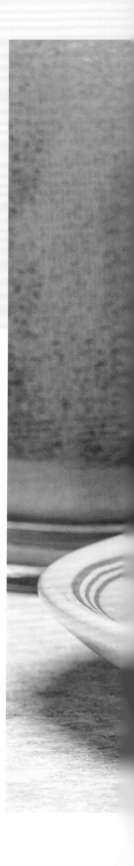

| | |
|---|---|
| 2 | jalapeño chiles, stemmed, seeded, and sliced into thin rings |
| 1 | cup red wine vinegar |
| ⅓ | cup sugar |
| ⅛ | teaspoon table salt |
| 1 | red onion, halved and sliced thin through root end |
| 1 | cup Barbecue Sauce (page 54) |
| 2 | cups shredded rotisserie chicken |
| 4 | hamburger buns |

**1** Microwave jalapeños, vinegar, sugar, and salt in medium bowl until simmering, 1 to 2 minutes. Stir in onion and let sit, stirring occasionally, for 45 minutes. Drain. (Drained pickled onions can be refrigerated for up to 1 week.)

**2** Bring barbecue sauce to simmer in medium saucepan over medium heat. Add chicken and cook until warmed through, 2 to 3 minutes. Serve chicken on buns with pickled red onions.

### Antoinette's Tip

You can use your favorite store-bought barbecue sauce, if you prefer.

# Coconut Green Curry Chicken Noodle Soup

**Serves:** 4 · **Total time:** 45 minutes

*This warming soup offers the wonderful flavors of Thai green curry with the convenience of store-bought curry paste and rotisserie chicken. I know, the ingredient list looks long, but the soup comes together quickly; plus, it's so delicious that I'm confident you will use up these ingredients making this soup again and again. The key to achieving the rich, creamy texture of this soup lies in using canned coconut milk. This luscious ingredient creates a velvety base that beautifully melds with the spices and other components of the dish. Using canned coconut milk (which is completely different from the refrigerated variety) ensures just the right consistency. The Indonesian sambal oelek chili paste adds a punch of heat to complement the creaminess of the coconut milk. You could substitute sriracha, though that will also add some sweetness.*

| | |
|---|---|
| 1 | tablespoon extra-virgin olive oil |
| 2 | carrots, peeled and sliced ¼ inch thick |
| 1 | red bell pepper, stemmed, seeded, and sliced thin |
| 1 | shallot, minced |
| 1 | teaspoon table salt |
| ½ | teaspoon pepper |
| 3 | scallions, sliced thin |
| 2 | tablespoons Thai green curry paste |
| 1 | tablespoon grated fresh ginger |
| 1 | teaspoon curry powder |
| 1 | teaspoon garlic powder |
| ½ | teaspoon ground allspice |
| 3 | cups chicken broth |
| 2 | tablespoons oyster sauce |
| 1 | tablespoon sambal oelek |
| 7 | ounces (¼-inch-wide) rice noodles |
| 2 | cups shredded rotisserie chicken |
| 1 | cup canned coconut milk |
| ¼ | cup fresh cilantro leaves |
| | Lime wedges |

**1** Heat oil in large saucepan over medium heat until shimmering. Add carrots, bell pepper, shallot, salt, and pepper and cook until peppers are just tender, about 5 minutes. Stir in scallions, curry paste, ginger, curry powder, garlic powder, and allspice and cook until fragrant, about 1 minute.

**2** Stir in broth, oyster sauce, and sambal oelek and bring to simmer over medium-high heat. Meanwhile, place noodles in large bowl, cover with boiling water, and let soak until almost tender, about 8 minutes, stirring occasionally. Drain noodles, rinse under cold running water, and drain well.

**3** Add noodles, chicken, and coconut milk to saucepan and return to simmer. Simmer until noodles are tender and chicken is warmed through, 3 to 5 minutes. Serve with cilantro and lime wedges.

# White Chicken Chili

**Serves:** 4 · **Total time:** 30 minutes

*While traditional chili typically features a rich, tomato-based sauce, white chicken chili takes
a departure from this norm. Its creamy base, made with ingredients including white beans,
chicken broth, and sometimes cream cheese, offers a velvety texture that is both comforting
and indulgent. Fresh cilantro brings a bright and herbaceous note, lifting the flavors and adding
a touch of freshness to each spoonful. Its distinct aroma and vibrant green color also add
visual appeal. Not only does this white chicken chili deliver a delightful flavor profile, but it also
offers the amazing ease of using store-bought rotisserie chicken, making it a breeze to prepare
in just half an hour. This shortcut ensures that you can enjoy a satisfying bowl of chili anytime,
without the hassle of longer cooking times or extra steps.*

2 tablespoons unsalted butter

1 small onion, chopped fine

⅓ cup minced celery

½ teaspoon table salt

½ teaspoon pepper

½ cup canned chopped green chiles

2 tablespoons all-purpose flour

3 cups chicken broth

2 cups shredded rotisserie chicken

1 (15-ounce) can cannellini beans, rinsed

2 ounces cream cheese, softened

1 teaspoon garlic powder

2 tablespoons chopped fresh cilantro, plus extra for serving

1 tablespoon lime juice, plus lime wedges for serving

Shredded Monterey Jack cheese

Tortilla chips

**1**  Melt butter in large saucepan over medium heat. Add onion, celery, salt, and pepper and cook until softened, 7 to 10 minutes. Stir in green chiles and flour and cook for 1 minute. Whisk in broth and bring to boil.

**2**  Add chicken, beans, cream cheese, and garlic powder, stirring until cream cheese is well combined and no lumps remain. Cook until warmed through, about 2 minutes. Stir in cilantro and lime juice and season with salt and pepper to taste. Serve with extra cilantro, lime wedges, shredded cheese, and tortilla chips.

## *Pantry Pick*

**Cannellini beans:** The creamy texture and mild flavor of these canned white beans round out this chili and also add character to soups, salads, and more. The test kitchen likes Goya Cannellini and Bush's Best Cannellini Beans.

### Antoinette's Tip

This chili tastes even better on day two! As it sits in the refrigerator, the ingredients meld together, creating a more complex flavor. So don't hesitate to double this recipe—the leftovers will reward you.

# Creamy Roasted Garlic and Chicken Pasta

**Serves:** 2 or 3 · **Total time:** 35 minutes

*Fresh rosemary, Pecorino Romano cheese, and store-bought rotisserie chicken are the heroes responsible for the majority of the flavor in this creamy chicken pasta. The fresh rosemary brings a piney earthiness, the Pecorino imparts a tangy and nutty dimension, and the chicken brings its juicy goodness. Roasted garlic is also a flavor powerhouse; you can use store-bought or make your own using the test kitchen's easy recipe. One of the great things about this recipe is that most of the ingredients are kitchen staples that many people already have on hand. I intentionally designed it this way because I firmly believe that creating delicious recipes doesn't always require an extensive list of ingredients. Sometimes—often, even—it just takes the right combination of simple ingredients to truly make a dish shine.*

| | |
|---|---|
| 8 | ounces penne |
| ¾ | teaspoon table salt, plus salt for cooking pasta |
| 2 | tablespoon unsalted butter |
| 2 | tablespoon all-purpose flour |
| 1 | tablespoon roasted garlic |
| 1 | teaspoon chopped fresh rosemary |
| 1 | cup heavy cream |
| 1 | teaspoon garlic powder |
| 2 | cups chopped rotisserie chicken |
| 1 | ounce Pecorino Romano cheese, grated (½ cup) |
| | Fresh parsley (optional) |

**1** Bring 2 quarts water to boil in large saucepan. Add pasta and 1½ teaspoons salt and cook, stirring often, until tender. Reserve 1½ cups cooking water, then drain pasta and set aside.

**2** Melt butter in 10-inch nonstick skillet over medium heat. Whisk in flour and cook for 2 minutes. Stir in roasted garlic and rosemary and cook until fragrant, about 30 seconds. Whisk in heavy cream, 1 cup reserved cooking water, garlic powder, and salt, whisking vigorously until well combined and smooth.

**3** Reduce heat to low; stir in chicken and cheese; and cook until cheese is melted and chicken is warmed through, about 1 minute. Add sauce to pasta in saucepan and toss to combine. Adjust consistency with remaining ½ cup reserved cooking water as needed. Serve, topped with parsley, if using.

# Roasted Garlic

**Makes:** 2 tablespoons
**Total time:** 30 minutes

1   large head garlic
½   teaspoon extra-virgin olive oil
    Pinch table salt

**1**   Remove outer papery skins from garlic. Cut off top third of head to expose cloves and discard. Place garlic head cut side up in center of large piece of aluminum foil, drizzle with oil, and sprinkle with salt. Gather foil tightly around garlic to form packet and place packet in air-fryer basket. Set temperature to 400 degrees, place basket in air fryer, and cook until garlic is soft and golden, about 20 minutes.

**2**   Carefully open packet to let garlic cool slightly. When cool enough to handle, squeeze cloves from skins; discard skins. (Whole head [pre-squeeze] can be refrigerated in airtight container for up to 1 week.)

## Antoinette's Tip

You can find prepared roasted garlic in the deli section of a well-stocked supermarket; if you can't find it, use the recipe here to make your own.

## Antoinette's Tip

You can substitute one red, orange, or yellow bell pepper, stemmed, seeded, and thinly sliced, for the frozen bell pepper strips.

# Mustard-Sesame Noodles

**Serves:** 4  ·  **Total time:** 45 minutes

*Chinese hot mustard, with its boldly spicy flavor, is the secret to these noodles. Unlike the milder yellow and brown mustards that take up lots of shelf space in the condiment aisle, Chinese mustard brings a distinctively sharp kick that invigorates the taste buds (see page 48 for more about Chinese mustard). For an umami-rich dressing, I combine the mustard with soy sauce, toasted sesame oil, rice vinegar, and a bit of sugar. Convenient frozen sliced bell peppers and a fresh carrot bring a vibrant burst of color as well as contributing to the overall flavor and texture, adding a subtle sweetness and satisfying crunch. And our good friend rotisserie chicken, shredded and stirred in with the veggies, makes this a meal.*

8   ounces fresh Chinese noodles

3   tablespoons Chinese hot mustard

3   tablespoons soy sauce

2   tablespoons toasted sesame oil

2   teaspoons unseasoned rice vinegar

½   teaspoon sugar

2   cups shredded rotisserie chicken

1   cup frozen bell pepper strips, thawed and patted dry

1   carrot, peeled and shredded

2   tablespoons chopped fresh cilantro

2   tablespoons toasted sesame seeds

**1**   Bring 4 quarts water to boil in large pot. Add noodles and cook, stirring often, until just tender. Drain noodles and rinse under cold running water until chilled; drain well.

**2**   Whisk mustard, soy sauce, oil, 1 tablespoon water, vinegar, and sugar together in large bowl. Add drained noodles, chicken, bell pepper, and carrot and toss to coat. Sprinkle with cilantro and sesame seeds and serve.

## *Pantry Pick*

**Fresh Chinese noodles:** Fresh Chinese noodles made from wheat and eggs boast a unique soft yet springy chewiness, and the uncooked noodles keep in the freezer for up to 1 month. There are a few different widths available; I usually buy lo mein noodles. I like the fresh noodles because they have such great texture, but if you can't find them, you can substitute dried lo mein noodles.

# Chicken Enchilada Bake

**Serves:** 4  ·  **Total time:** 1¼ hours

*Preparing this dish is a cinch, thanks to the thoughtful use of rotisserie chicken and canned ingredients. Rather than relying on store-bought enchilada sauce, which can be a little lacking, I've crafted a bright-tasting homemade version that literally takes about 30 seconds to make. By blending seasoned diced tomatoes and green chiles with smoky adobo chiles and lime juice, you end up with a robust sauce that coats the chicken with a perfect balance of tanginess and spice. Building the bake is like assembling a lasagna, but simpler; just layer the saucy chicken with corn tortillas and shredded Monterey Jack cheese into a baking pan. The final sprinkle of cheese on top melts into a golden blanket of gooey deliciousness in the oven.*

2   (10-ounce) cans Ro-Tel Original Diced Tomatoes & Green Chilies, drained

2   tablespoons minced canned chipotle chile in adobo sauce

2   tablespoons lime juice

½   teaspoon table salt

2   cups shredded rotisserie chicken

8   (6-inch) flour tortillas, divided

8   ounces Monterey Jack cheese, shredded (2 cups), divided

Sour cream

Cilantro

**1** Adjust oven rack to middle position and heat oven to 400 degrees. Process tomatoes, chipotle, lime juice, and salt in food processor until smooth, about 20 seconds. Transfer to bowl and stir in chicken.

**2** Spray 8-inch square baking pan with vegetable oil spray. Spread one-third of chicken mixture over bottom of prepared pan. Arrange 4 tortillas over chicken mixture, overlapping tortillas in center of pan and pressing tortillas into corners and up sides of pan. Spread one-third of chicken mixture over tortillas in pan, then sprinkle with half of Monterey Jack. Repeat with remaining 4 tortillas, remaining chicken mixture, and remaining cheese.

**3** Bake uncovered until sauce is bubbling and cheese is golden brown, about 30 minutes. Let cool for 10 minutes. Serve with sour cream and cilantro.

## *Pantry Pick*

**Ro-Tel Original Diced Tomatoes & Green Chilies:** Thank you, Carl Roettele, for creating this must-have canned good in Texas, way back in the 1940s. It rapidly became an essential ingredient in Texas queso dip and these days brings its zesty, fire-roasted flavor to all kinds of dishes, Tex-Mex or otherwise.

# Mini Chicken Pot Pies

**Serves:** 10 to 12 (makes 30 pot pies)  ·  **Total time:** 35 minutes

*This crowd-pleasing appetizer is a winner for entertaining because it looks impressively elegant but takes barely more than half an hour to make, thanks to the convenience of mini phyllo dough cups, rotisserie chicken, and frozen vegetables. The creamy base of the pot pie filling relies on the magic of cream of mushroom soup. This classic pantry staple works wonders, providing a velvety texture and rich flavor. Sautéed shallot and garlic and a medley of herbs add depth and complexity. The shredded rotisserie chicken brings succulent heartiness, while the vegetable medley adds pops of color and flavor. A touch of lemon juice brightens up the filling. As you bake these mini pot pies, the phyllo cups turn beautifully golden and crisp, creating a delightful contrast to the creamy filling. Your guests will be wowed by this app that encapsulates the comfort of a classic chicken pot pie in a perfectly portioned form.*

| | |
|---|---|
| 1 | tablespoon unsalted butter |
| 1 | small shallot, minced |
| 1 | garlic clove, minced |
| ¼ | teaspoon dried rosemary |
| ¼ | teaspoon dried thyme |
| ¼ | teaspoon table salt |
| ⅛ | teaspoon pepper |
| 1½ | cups shredded rotisserie chicken |
| 1 | (10.5-ounce) can cream of mushroom soup |
| ¾ | cup frozen carrot, corn, and green bean medley, thawed |
| ½ | teaspoon lemon juice |
| 2 | (1.9-ounce) boxes phyllo shells |

**1**    Adjust oven rack to middle position and heat oven to 350 degrees. Melt butter in medium saucepan over medium heat. Add shallot and cook until softened, about 3 minutes. Add garlic, rosemary, thyme, salt, and pepper and cook until fragrant, 30 seconds to 1 minute. Stir in chicken, cream of mushroom soup, and vegetable medley and simmer over low heat until vegetables are warmed through, 3 to 5 minutes. Remove from heat and stir in lemon juice.

**2**    Arrange phyllo shells in single layer on rimmed baking sheet and bake until crisp, about 5 minutes. Carefully fill each phyllo shell with 1 rounded tablespoon filling, then return to oven and bake until warmed through, about 5 minutes. Serve.

## *Pantry Pick*

**Phyllo shells:** Tissue-thin, flaky, crispy phyllo is a taste treat, but working with phyllo sheets can be frustrating and doesn't lend itself to speed. Enter frozen phyllo shells. These little cups are so convenient—they just need a short prebake to prep them. They're just begging to be filled with practically anything your imagination can dream up.

### Antoinette's Tip

I give suggested dimensions for the burger size, but you should match the size of the bread you're using; just be sure to adjust your cooking time in step 3 accordingly. I recommend making the patties slightly larger than the bread, because they will shrink in size as they cook.

# Pesto Cheeseburgers

**Serves:** 4    ·    **Total time:** 40 minutes

*At this point in the chapter, we turn our attention from rotisserie chicken to another of my all-time favorite supermarket prepared foods: refrigerated pesto (see page 103 for more information about this must-have ingredient). We all know that pesto is a pasta lover's best friend, but it can work its magic on many other foods as well. Let's start with these burgers. This recipe is all about maximizing flavor and minimizing waste by repurposing that open container of pesto that might be sitting in your fridge. Mixing pesto into burgers adds not only flavor but also moisture to help ensure juicy patties. Pressing a divot into the center of the patties is a great test-kitchen trick to make sure the patties stay flat and don't dome up while they're cooking. These rich burgers pair perfectly with a quick, brightly acidic tomato jam, mellowed by the mild and melty mozzarella.*

1   tablespoon unsalted butter

1   tablespoon plus 1 teaspoon extra-virgin olive oil, divided

10   ounces grape tomatoes

1   teaspoon table salt, divided

3   garlic cloves, peeled

2   sprigs fresh thyme

1   teaspoon white wine vinegar

½   teaspoon granulated sugar

⅛   teaspoon pepper

1½   pounds 80 percent lean ground beef

¾   cup pesto

8   ounces fresh mozzarella cheese, sliced ¼ inch thick

8   slices French bread, lightly toasted

**1**   Heat butter and 1 tablespoon oil in small saucepan over medium-high heat until butter is melted. Add tomatoes and ½ teaspoon salt and cook until tomatoes begin to burst, about 3 minutes. Add garlic and thyme sprigs; reduce heat to low; and cook until all tomatoes have burst, about 2 minutes. Off heat, discard thyme sprigs and garlic and stir in vinegar, sugar, and pepper. Set aside.

**2**   Combine beef, pesto, and remaining ½ teaspoon salt in bowl, kneading with your hands until well combined. Divide beef mixture into 4 equal portions, then gently shape each portion into 3½-inch-wide by 5-inch-long oval. Using your fingertips, press center of each patty down until about ½ inch thick, creating slight divot.

**3**   Heat remaining 1 teaspoon oil in 12-inch skillet over medium heat until just smoking. Transfer patties to skillet, divot side up, and cook until well browned on first side, 2 to 4 minutes. Flip patties, top with mozzarella, and continue to cook until browned on second side and meat registers 120 to 125 degrees (for medium-rare) or 130 to 135 degrees (for medium), 3 to 5 minutes. Transfer burgers to platter and let rest for 5 minutes.

**4**   Divide reserved tomato mixture evenly among 4 slices bread. Top with burgers and remaining bread and serve.

# Air-Fried Pesto Chicken Roll-Ups

**Serves:** 2 · **Total time:** 45 minutes

*Get ready for a flavor-packed and hassle-free meal that's pretty enough to serve to guests. These delectable chicken roll-ups are all about simplicity and bold taste (they look impressive too). Take a juicy chicken breast, slather it with store-bought refrigerated pesto, layer it with sun-dried tomatoes and fresh mozzarella, and roll it up into a delightful package that will please everyone at the table. The use of fresh mozzarella is crucial here, as it adds a creamy, melty goodness that really complements the pesto and tomatoes. So get rolling and enjoy the incredible flavors of these chicken roll-ups.*

½  teaspoon table salt

½  teaspoon garlic powder

½  teaspoon pepper

4  ounces fresh mozzarella cheese, shredded (1 cup)

½  cup pesto, divided

2  tablespoons chopped sun-dried tomatoes

½  cup panko bread crumbs

2  (6- to 8-ounce) boneless, skinless chicken breasts, trimmed

1  tablespoon lemon juice

**1**   Combine salt, garlic powder, and pepper in bowl. Combine mozzarella, ¼ cup pesto, and tomatoes in second bowl. Place panko in shallow dish.

**2**   Working with 1 chicken breast at a time, starting on thick side, cut chicken in half horizontally (you should have 2 thin, nearly identical-looking pieces). Arrange chicken in single layer on cutting board, cover with plastic wrap, and pound until ¼ to ½ inch thick. Discard plastic and pat chicken dry with paper towels.

**3**   Sprinkle salt mixture evenly over both sides of chicken. Divide mozzarella mixture among chicken halves, spreading to cover evenly. Starting at narrowest end, tightly roll chicken halves away from you into tight roll-up; place roll-ups seam side down on cutting board. Brush tops of chicken roll-ups with 2 tablespoons pesto, then dredge coated side in panko, pressing gently to adhere.

**4**   Place chicken roll-ups in air fryer basket, coated side up. Place basket in air fryer and set temperature to 400 degrees. Cook until panko is golden and center of roll-ups register 160 degrees, about 15 minutes. Transfer chicken to serving dish and let rest for 5 minutes. Combine remaining 2 tablespoons pesto with lemon juice and drizzle over chicken. Serve.

## Antoinette's Tip

This recipe is written to serve one person, but it can be easily scaled to serve up to four people with four salmon fillets. All you need to do is make an 8-inch-wide foil sling in step 1 to accommodate four fillets.

# Air-Fried Pesto Salmon Fillet

**Serves:** 1 · **Total time:** 25 minutes

*Bid farewell to boring salmon with this pesto-licious fillet. As I was developing this recipe, I wanted to put a flavorful twist on the usual air-fried salmon fillet, which has become a dinnertime mainstay but can sometimes feel pretty mundane. With a simple seasoning of salt and pepper, a generous slather of refrigerated store-bought pesto, and a delectable bread-crumb and parsley topping, this salmon fillet bursts with flavors that will remind you of a fine-dining experience. With the help of the air fryer, achieving these restaurant-quality results has never been easier.*

2 tablespoons panko bread crumbs

1 teaspoon chopped fresh parsley

1 (6- to 8-ounce) skinless salmon fillet, 1½ inches thick

⅛ teaspoon table salt

⅛ teaspoon pepper

2 tablespoons pesto

**1**   Make foil sling for air-fryer basket by folding 1 long sheet of aluminum foil so it is 4 inches wide. Lay sheet of foil widthwise across basket, pressing foil into and up sides of basket. Fold excess foil as needed so that edges of foil are flush with top of basket.

**2**   Transfer panko to shallow dish and stir in parsley. Pat salmon dry with paper towels and sprinkle with salt and pepper. Brush top of salmon with pesto, then dredge coated side in panko mixture, pressing gently to adhere. Arrange fillet coated side up on sling in prepared basket.

**3**   Place basket in air fryer and set temperature to 400 degrees. Cook until salmon is still translucent when checked with tip of paring knife and registers 125 degrees (for medium-rare), 10 to 14 minutes, using sling to rotate fillet halfway through cooking. Using sling, carefully remove salmon from air fryer. Serve.

## *Pantry Pick*

**Pesto:** Store-bought refrigerated pesto is a flavor key that opens many doors. Besides slathering this salmon with it, in this chapter I also use it in burger patties and chicken roll-ups and to stuff mushrooms. You can spread it on pizza, toss it with roasted potatoes, and of course use it on pasta! For the best flavor, buy pesto made with extra-virgin olive oil. The test kitchen likes Buitoni Pesto with Basil.

# Pesto-Stuffed Mushrooms

**Serves:** 4 to 6 as an appetizer · **Total time:** 35 minutes

*There are certain finger foods that I can never pass up. Mini quiches are one (see Carbonara Quiche Cups on page 156), and stuffed mushrooms are another. For years I would only indulge in these treats if I were at an event or a restaurant, but I never thought to make them at home. It wasn't until I had some leftover refrigerated pesto and some mushrooms that were on the brink of breaking down that I decided to experiment and create my own version. To ensure even cooking, make sure you select mushrooms that are similar in size. I prefer mushrooms that are about 1 inch wide, because they create a perfect one-bite appetizer.*

8   ounces cremini mushrooms, each about 1 inch wide, trimmed

1   teaspoon plus 2 tablespoons pesto, divided

1   shallot, minced

2   tablespoon panko bread crumbs

2   tablespoon finely grated Pecorino Romano cheese

1   tablespoon extra-virgin olive oil

⅛   teaspoon table salt

⅛   teaspoon pepper

**1**   Adjust oven rack to middle position and heat oven to 375 degrees. Line rimmed baking sheet with aluminum foil and spray with vegetable oil spray. Remove stems from mushrooms and chop fine. Set mushroom caps aside. Cook 1 teaspoon pesto and shallot in 10-inch nonstick skillet over medium heat, stirring constantly, until shallot is softened, about 2 minutes. Add chopped mushroom stems and cook until softened, about 3 minutes. Off heat, stir in remaining 2 tablespoons pesto; transfer to bowl and set aside.

**2**   Wipe out skillet. Toast panko in now-empty skillet over medium-high heat, stirring frequently, until golden, 3 to 5 minutes. Remove from heat and stir in Pecorino.

**3**   Toss reserved mushroom caps, oil, salt, and pepper together in bowl. Arrange mushroom caps stem side up on prepared sheet. Stuff each mushroom with reserved pesto-mushroom mixture, then sprinkle evenly with panko-Pecorino mixture. Bake mushrooms until softened and cheese is melted, 10 to 15 minutes. Serve.

## *Pantry Pick*

**Panko bread crumbs:** This Japanese style of bread crumbs is made from steamed, crust-free bread that's processed into dried flakes. They're larger and flakier than American-style bread crumbs, so they make crispier toppings and lighter meatballs and meatloaf. The test kitchen likes Kikkoman Panko Bread Crumbs.

## Antoinette's Tip

You can use larger (or smaller) mushrooms, though you'll need to adjust the baking time in step 3 accordingly.

# Herbed Goat Cheese Scramble

**Serves:** 1 · **Total time:** 10 minutes

*Seasoned goat cheese logs are another prepared food that I recommend keeping in your refrigerator—the cheese and the seasoning are wrapped in one convenient package. In this velvety version of a classic egg scramble, creamy-tangy goat cheese with garlic and herbs takes center stage. The simple yet proven technique for cooking the eggs and the combination of just a few flavorful ingredients create a symphony of textures and tastes. By repurposing the last bits of a leftover log of goat cheese, you can add a luxurious twist that transforms an ordinary scramble into a memorable meal. You can easily double this recipe using a 10-inch nonstick skillet, or even make 4 servings in a 12-inch skillet.*

| | |
|---|---|
| 2 | large eggs |
| 1 | tablespoon heavy cream |
| ⅛ | teaspoon table salt |
| | Pinch pepper |
| 1½ | teaspoons unsalted butter |
| 2 | tablespoons crumbled garlic and herb goat cheese |

**1** Beat eggs, cream, salt, and pepper in bowl with fork until eggs are thoroughly combined.

**2** Melt butter in 8-inch nonstick skillet over medium-high heat, swirling to coat pan. Add egg mixture and, using rubber spatula, constantly and firmly scrape along bottom and sides of skillet until eggs begin to clump and spatula leaves trail on bottom of skillet, 30 seconds to 1 minute.

**3** Reduce heat to low and sprinkle goat cheese over top. Gently but constantly fold eggs until clumped and slightly wet, 30 to 60 seconds. Transfer eggs to plate and serve immediately.

## *Pantry Pick*

### Garlic and herb goat cheese:

Logs of fresh goat cheese have mild but bright flavors. You might think of this style of goat cheese as something you only eat uncooked, spread on crackers or crumbled over salad, but it melds beautifully with eggs or pizza or pasta.

### Antoinette's Tip

You can substitute half-and-half for the heavy cream, or even use milk if that is what you have on hand.

# Butternut Squash and Parmesan Soup

**Serves:** 4 to 6   ·   **Total time:** 40 minutes

*Already peeled and chopped and ready to go to work, frozen winter squash is an unsung hero of the frozen food aisle. Here's a squash soup that's quick but tastes like it's been simmered for hours. While many butternut squash soup recipes lean into sweetness, this one takes a different route by infusing the soup with decidedly savory flavors. The combination of fennel, garlic, tomato paste, chicken broth, wine, and Parmesan creates a blend of aromas and tastes that offset the inherent sweetness of the butternut squash. As you blend the cooked squash mixture to a velvety smooth consistency, the flavors all come together. The Parmesan adds a nutty and salty finishing note, melting into the soup to add creamy texture and depth of flavor.*

| | |
|---|---|
| 2 | tablespoons unsalted butter |
| 1 | fennel bulb, stalks discarded, bulb halved, cored, and cut into ½-inch pieces |
| 1½ | teaspoons table salt |
| 3 | garlic cloves, minced |
| 2 | teaspoons tomato paste |
| ¼ | teaspoon pepper |
| ⅛ | teaspoon ground allspice |
| 24 | ounces frozen butternut squash pieces |
| 2 | cups chicken broth |
| ½ | cup dry white wine |
| ½ | cup water |
| 1 | bay leaf |
| 1⅓ | ounces Parmesan cheese, grated (⅔ cup), plus extra for serving |
| 1 | tablespoon chopped fresh parsley |

**1**   Melt butter in large saucepan over medium heat. Add fennel and salt and cook until softened, about 5 minutes. Stir in garlic, tomato paste, pepper, and allspice and cook until fragrant, about 30 seconds. Stir in squash, broth, wine, water, and bay leaf, scraping up any browned bits, and bring to simmer over medium-high heat. Reduce heat to medium-low and simmer until squash is very tender, 5 to 7 minutes.

**2**   Discard bay leaf. Working in batches, process soup in blender (or use immersion blender) until smooth, 30 seconds to 1 minute. Return soup to saucepan, stir in Parmesan, and season with salt and pepper to taste. Serve, sprinkling with parsley and passing extra Parmesan separately.

## Pantry Pick

**Frozen butternut squash:** I can't overstate the convenience of using frozen butternut squash pieces, whether in this soup or just as a quick roasted side dish. By bypassing the laborious task of peeling, seeding, and chopping a whole squash, you save valuable time in the kitchen.

# Chicken Gnocchi Soup

**Serves:** 4 · **Total time:** 30 minutes

*This twist on classic chicken noodle soup brings together the convenience of store-bought gnocchi and the succulent flavors and ease of rotisserie chicken. I wanted to create a shortcut that makes chicken soup not only easier but also much quicker to prepare, ensuring that anyone can have a warm and satisfying bowl in front of them in no time. The pillowy yet hearty gnocchi effortlessly absorb the flavors of the broth, and the shreds of tender chicken add richness without having to undergo a long simmer. This soup recipe is one of my go-to quick fixes when I'm craving a comforting bowl of soup but don't want to spend hours in the kitchen.*

| | |
|---|---|
| 1 | tablespoon extra-virgin olive oil |
| 1 | shallot, minced |
| 1 | celery rib, chopped fine |
| 1 | carrot, peeled and shredded |
| ¼ | teaspoon table salt |
| ½ | teaspoon pepper |
| 2 | garlic cloves, minced |
| ½ | teaspoon dried thyme |
| 3½ | cups chicken broth |
| 1 | pound shelf-stable potato gnocchi |
| 2 | cups chopped rotisserie chicken |
| ½ | cup frozen peas |

**1**  Heat oil in medium saucepan over medium heat until shimmering. Add shallot, celery, carrot, salt, and pepper and cook until vegetables are softened, 5 to 8 minutes. Stir in garlic and thyme and cook until fragrant, about 30 seconds.

**2**  Stir in broth and bring to boil over medium-high heat. Add gnocchi, reduce heat to medium, and cook until tender, 3 to 4 minutes. Stir in chicken and peas and cook until warmed through, about 2 minutes. Serve.

## *Pantry Pick*

**Shelf-stable gnocchi:** This pantry wonder is fully cooked and doesn't need to be boiled before using, unlike frozen or refrigerated store-bought gnocchi. It also has a lower moisture content than refrigerated or frozen gnocchi, so I think it's easier to work with, staying firmer and holding up better to high heat.

# Air-Fried Crispy Gnocchi with Artichokes

**Serves:** 2 or 3  ·  **Total time:** 30 minutes

*By utilizing ingredients you can easily store in your pantry, you can create a dish that feels gourmet with minimal effort. The secret to achieving the heavenly texture of these gnocchi lies in the air fryer, which transforms them into delightful morsels that are crispy on the outside but tender and pillowy on the inside. It's a textural sensation that will have you reaching for bite after bite. For a quick hit of flavor with tangy acidity, I pair the gnocchi with canned artichoke hearts. They go into the air fryer too, turning golden and slightly crispy alongside the gnocchi. Parmesan cheese and fresh basil finish this dish off in style.*

- 1   pound shelf-stable potato gnocchi
- 1   (14-ounce) can artichoke hearts, rinsed, patted dry, and quartered, plus 2 tablespoons brine
- 2   tablespoons extra-virgin olive oil, plus extra for drizzling
- ½   teaspoon garlic powder
- ½   teaspoon table salt
- ¼   teaspoon pepper
- ¼   cup grated Parmesan cheese, plus extra for serving
- 2   tablespoons chopped fresh basil

**1**   Toss gnocchi, artichoke hearts, oil, garlic powder, salt, and pepper together in bowl; transfer to air-fryer basket.

**2**   Place basket in air fryer and set temperature to 400 degrees. Cook until gnocchi and artichokes are golden brown, about 20 minutes, stirring halfway through.

**3**   Return gnocchi mixture to now-empty bowl and toss with artichoke brine, Parmesan, and basil. Transfer to serving platter and drizzle with extra oil and sprinkle with extra Parmesan. Serve.

### Antoinette's Tip

Be sure to use shelf-stable (not refrigerated or frozen) gnocchi. Separate any stuck-together gnocchi before tossing with the oil in step 1.

## Antoinette's Tip

Be sure to use shelf-stable (not refrigerated or frozen)
gnocchi in this recipe. Separate any stuck-together
gnocchi before adding them to the skillet in step 2.

# Crispy Gnocchi with Roasted Red Pepper Sauce

**Serves:** 2 or 3 · **Total time:** 25 minutes

*As an avid lover of sauces of all kinds, I am thrilled to share this easy and irresistible dish that showcases the magic of roasted red peppers. One of my favorite ways to elevate a dish is by creating a velvety sauce with these jarred gems. The process is incredibly simple, requiring just a blender and a few other ingredients. Here, olive oil, tomato paste, garlic powder, and Italian seasoning contribute to the vibrant, tangy-sweet, slightly smoky sauce that perfectly coats the gnocchi. I turn to the stovetop to crisp up the gnocchi in this recipe, sizzling them in olive oil until they develop a deep golden crust before stirring in the aromatic sauce to finish.*

¾ cup jarred roasted red peppers

¼ cup extra-virgin olive oil, divided

2 tablespoons warm tap water

2 tablespoons tomato paste

½ teaspoon garlic powder

½ teaspoon Italian seasoning blend

½ teaspoon pepper

1 pound shelf-stable potato gnocchi

1 tablespoon chopped fresh parsley

**1** Process red peppers, 2 tablespoons oil, water, tomato paste, garlic powder, Italian seasoning, and pepper in blender until smooth, about 60 seconds, scraping down sides of blender jar as needed.

**2** Heat remaining 2 tablespoons oil in 12-inch nonstick skillet over medium-high heat until shimmering. Add gnocchi in single layer and cook, without moving, until well browned and crispy on one side, about 6 minutes. Stir gnocchi and continue to cook until just beginning to brown on second side, about 2 minutes. Remove skillet from heat, add red pepper sauce, and stir until gnocchi are well coated. (If sauce is too thick, add additional warm water, 1 tablespoon at a time, until sauce reaches desired consistency.) Sprinkle with parsley and serve.

## *Pantry Pick*

### Jarred roasted red peppers:

Packed in a brine of water, salt, and sometimes vinegar and olive oil, sweet, smoky jarred roasted red bell peppers are a huge timesaver over roasting fresh peppers. An open jar keeps for weeks in the fridge, but you'll be using them up before then in salads, omelets, and more. The test kitchen likes Cento Roasted Peppers.

# Weeknight Ravioli Lasagna

**Serves:** 4 to 6  ·  **Total time:** 1½ hours

*Here's my liberty-taking, lazy, yet utterly delicious twist on traditional lasagna. By using frozen ravioli, this recipe eliminates the need for fiddling with lasagna noodles and a separate ricotta mixture—the cheese is already built into the pasta, and you don't even need to thaw the ravioli before baking. The simple sauce starts with store-bought marinara and incorporates two secret weapons. First, red wine is a game-changer when incorporated into sauces. As it reduces, much of the alcohol evaporates, leaving behind concentrated flavors. Second, as I learned from the test kitchen, adding anchovies to sauces enhances flavor without tasting fishy. These small but mighty fish lend umami richness to this marinara. And the mozzarella and Parmesan add even more cheesy goodness—what we all want from a good lasagna.*

1  tablespoon extra-virgin olive oil

1  shallot, minced

2  garlic cloves, minced

3  anchovy fillets, minced

¼  cup red wine

1  (24-ounce) jar marinara sauce

2  tablespoons chopped fresh parsley

4  ounces whole-milk block mozzarella cheese, shredded (1 cup)

1½  ounces Parmesan cheese, shredded (½ cup)

20  ounces square frozen cheese ravioli

**1**   Adjust oven rack to middle position and heat oven to 400 degrees. Heat oil in medium saucepan over medium heat until shimmering. Add shallot and cook until softened, about 3 minutes. Add garlic and anchovies and cook until fragrant, about 30 seconds. Stir in wine and cook until evaporated, scraping up any browned bits, about 3 minutes. Stir in marinara and parsley and remove from heat.

**2**   Combine mozzarella and Parmesan cheeses in bowl. Spread ¾ cup sauce in bottom of 8-inch square baking pan. Arrange half of ravioli in even layer on sauce. Repeat layering of ¾ cup sauce and remaining ravioli, then top with remaining sauce. Sprinkle evenly with cheese mixture. Cover tightly with greased aluminum foil and bake until bubbling and cheese is melted, about 40 minutes. Remove foil and continue to cook uncovered until cheese is lightly browned, about 15 minutes (7 minutes if using refrigerated ravioli). Let cool on wire rack for 10 minutes. Serve.

## *Pantry Pick*

**Frozen ravioli:** Keeping a bag of frozen ravioli in the freezer means you always have a quick meal when you need one. Frozen ravioli are usually less expensive than refrigerated ravioli, but you can substitute a refrigerated variety, if you prefer.

## Antoinette's Tips

Larger ravioli (about 2½ inches wide, sometimes called jumbo ravioli) create more visible lasagna-like layers. If you can't find larger ravioli, smaller ravioli will work, but the layers will be less prominent.

Not every timesaver is worth it. Preshredded cheese is coated with additives to keep it from clumping, which can affect its meltability. Now, it's not like I never buy this convenience product, but for this lasagna, I like the melty mouthfeel that comes with shredding a block of mozzarella.

### Antoinette's Tip

When I can, I make this a day ahead, since the flavors become even more robust after a little time in the fridge!

# Tortellini Salad

**Serves:** 2 as a main or 4 as a side    ·    **Total time:** 50 minutes

*No matter what kind of pasta you're using, achieving the perfect texture is the key to a delicious pasta salad. Here are my tips for cooking frozen cheese tortellini just right for this dish: First, whatever brand you choose, follow the cooking instructions carefully. Second, test for doneness frequently. As the tortellini cook, they will start to float to the top of the boiling water. Carefully remove a single tortellini from the top of the water, cut off a bit of the pasta, and taste it. The pasta should be tender but still have a slight bite (al dente). If it's too firm, continue cooking for an additional minute or two, then test again. Third, avoid overcooking by immediately rinsing the drained tortellini under cold water. Beyond that, the beauty of this recipe lies in its simplicity. With just a few flavorful pantry ingredients—olive oil, wine vinegar, olives, and Parmesan—plus cherry tomatoes and some fresh herbs, you can whip up this scrumptious—and portable—meal in no time.*

| | |
|---|---|
| 12 | ounces frozen cheese tortellini |
| ½ | teaspoon table salt, plus salt for cooking pasta |
| ⅓ | cup extra-virgin olive oil |
| 2 | tablespoons white wine vinegar |
| ¼ | teaspoon pepper |
| 3 | ounces cherry tomatoes, halved |
| ½ | cup large pitted Castelvetrano olives, halved |
| ¼ | cup chopped fresh parsley |
| 3 | tablespoons grated Parmesan cheese |
| 1 | tablespoon shredded fresh basil |

**1**   Bring 4 quarts water to boil in large pot. Add pasta and 1 tablespoon salt and cook, stirring often, until tender. Meanwhile, whisk oil, vinegar, salt, and pepper together in medium bowl. Drain pasta and rinse under cold running water until chilled; drain well. Transfer to bowl with dressing.

**2**   Add tomatoes and olives to bowl with pasta and toss to combine. Stir in parsley, Parmesan, and basil. Serve.

## *Pantry Pick*

**Frozen tortellini:** I stash my bag of frozen tortellini right next to my bag of frozen ravioli. They lend themselves perfectly to pasta salads like this one, and their adorable belly button shape makes them just as family-friendly as ravioli.

# Chapter 4

# Instant Pot Assets

Instant Pot Baked Potato Soup

Instant Pot Barbecue Burnt Ends

Instant Pot Roast

Instant Pot Beef Ragu

Instant Pot Quesabirria Tacos

Instant Pot Barbecue Ribs

Instant Pot Carolina-Style Pulled Pork

Instant Pot Cajun-Inspired
Shrimp and Rice

Instant Pot Collard Greens

# Instant Pot Baked Potato Soup

**Serves:** 4 to 6   ·   **Total time:** 1¼ hours

*Imagine all the starchy, cheesy, meaty flavors of a loaded baked potato transformed into a creamy, hearty soup that will comfort your soul on a cold night. With the magic of the Instant Pot, you'll expend very little effort on the way to enjoying this delicious soup. Not only does it capture the essence of a classic loaded potato, but I take it up another notch by also sautéing the leeks (right in the pot) in the savory goodness of the fat left from cooking the bacon. The combination of rich potatoes and cheddar; smoky bacon; and delicately sweet leeks creates a symphony of flavors that will keep you dipping your spoon into the bowl. To keep the bacon crispy, I sprinkle it on top for garnish, along with scallions for a fresh flavor burst.*

| | |
|---|---|
| 6 | slices bacon, chopped fine |
| 1½ | pounds leeks, white and light green parts only, halved lengthwise, sliced thin, and washed thoroughly |
| 2 | teaspoons table salt, divided |
| 4 | garlic cloves, minced |
| ½ | teaspoon ground allspice |
| 2 | pounds russet potatoes, peeled and cut into 1-inch pieces |
| 2¼ | cups chicken broth |
| ¾ | cup white wine |
| ½ | cup heavy cream |
| 4 | ounces sharp cheddar cheese, grated (1 cup) |
| 2 | scallions, sliced thin |

**1** Using highest sauté function, cook bacon in Instant Pot until crispy, about 10 minutes. Use slotted spoon to remove bacon, leaving fat behind, and transfer to paper towel–lined plate; set aside until ready to serve. Add leeks and 1 teaspoon salt to fat left in pot and cook until softened, 8 to 10 minutes.

**2** Add garlic and allspice and cook until fragrant, about 30 seconds. Stir in potatoes, broth, wine, and cream, scraping up any browned bits. Lock lid into place and close pressure-release valve. Select high pressure-cook function and cook for 25 minutes.

**3** Turn off Instant Pot and quick-release pressure. Carefully remove lid, allowing steam to escape away from you. Working in batches, process soup in blender (or use immersion blender) until smooth, about 2 minutes. Return soup to pot and stir in cheese and remaining 1 teaspoon salt. Sprinkle with reserved bacon and scallions and serve.

## Pantry Pick

**Bacon:** I'm a big fan of purchasing precooked bacon at the supermarket for its convenience, but sometimes there's an advantage to using regular bacon. In this recipe, you sauté the leeks in the flavorful fat left in the Instant Pot after crisping up the bacon.

# Instant Pot Barbecue Burnt Ends

**Serves:** 2  ·  **Total time:** 1¼ hours

*This recipe changed my life. For the final challenge on America's Test Kitchen: The Next Generation, I impressed the judges enough with my easy burnt ends that I won the competition! These melt-in-your-mouth nuggets of goodness are a barbecue lover's dream come true—and they made my food dreams come true. Burnt ends usually start with a huge slab of beef brisket and require hours in a smoker. Here, I layer smoky flavor into more affordable beef chuck-eye with a zesty homemade spice rub, a rich homemade barbecue sauce, and some liquid smoke. I was able to shorten the cooking time drastically by harnessing the magic of the Instant Pot and achieve the "burnt" part by running the tender meat under the broiler, allowing you to enjoy these irresistible burnt ends without the long hours of smoking. This is one of my favorite recipes because it lets anyone experience the best of barbecue flavors without having to own a smoker or grill or order from a restaurant.*

1 (1½-pound) boneless beef chuck-eye roast, trimmed and cut into 1½-inch pieces

¼ cup plus 2 tablespoons Barbecue Spice Rub, divided (page 55)

½ teaspoon table salt

1 tablespoon vegetable oil

1 cup water

½ cup Barbecue Sauce, divided (page 54)

1 tablespoon Worcestershire sauce

1 tablespoon cider vinegar

½ teaspoon liquid smoke

2 tablespoons packed dark brown sugar

Pickled Vegetables (page 19)

**1**  Pat beef dry with paper towels, then sprinkle with ¼ cup barbecue spice rub and salt, turning to coat evenly. Using highest sauté function, heat oil in Instant Pot until shimmering. Add beef and cook until browned all over, 4 minutes. Stir in water, ¼ cup barbecue sauce, Worcestershire, cider vinegar, and liquid smoke. Lock lid into place and close pressure-release valve. Select high pressure-cook function and cook for 30 minutes.

**2**  Adjust oven rack 6 inches from broiler element and heat broiler. Line rimmed baking sheet with aluminum foil. Combine sugar and remaining 2 tablespoons barbecue spice rub in medium bowl. Turn off Instant Pot and quick-release pressure. Carefully remove lid, allowing steam to escape away from you. Using spider skimmer or slotted spoon, transfer beef to bowl with sugar mixture, and stir to coat. Transfer beef to center of prepared sheet in single layer with no space between pieces.

**3**  Broil beef until beginning to char in spots, 4 to 6 minutes. Return beef to bowl, add remaining ¼ cup barbecue sauce, and stir to coat. Serve with pickles.

# Instant Pot Roast

**Serves:** 6 · **Total time:** 1½ hours, plus 15 minutes resting

*Classic pot roast can take 3 hours, and often longer, in the oven, but in this recipe you'll take a beef chuck-eye roast to a whole new level of juicy deliciousness in record time. Chuck-eye is a continuation of the muscles that form the rib eye (one of the most flavorful and tender beef cuts), and with low amounts of fat to trim off, it offers a high yield of meat for your money. So picture this: perfectly roasted marbled beef, so soft it practically falls apart with a single touch, with fork-tender potatoes and carrots surrounding it on the platter, family-style. But we're not stopping there, y'all. We're bringing in some serious flavor with not one, but two, secret weapons: red wine and beef broth. Oh, yes! These ingredients really work their magic under pressure, infusing every bite with richness and deep flavor.*

2   teaspoons pepper

2   teaspoons minced fresh rosemary
    or thyme

1½  teaspoons table salt

½   teaspoon garlic powder

3   pounds boneless beef chuck-eye
    roast, trimmed

2   tablespoons extra-virgin olive oil,
    divided

1   onion, sliced thin

2   celery ribs, chopped

4   garlic cloves, minced

¼   cup red wine

6   (8-ounce) Yukon Gold potatoes,
    peeled and halved crosswise

1   pound carrots, peeled and cut into
    2-inch lengths

1   cup beef broth

2   tablespoons Worcestershire sauce

**1**   Combine pepper, rosemary, salt, and garlic powder in bowl. Pat beef dry with paper towels then rub all over with pepper mixture. Using highest sauté function, heat 1 tablespoon oil in Instant Pot until shimmering. Add beef and brown on all sides, 10 to 12 minutes. Transfer to large plate. Add remaining 1 tablespoon oil, onion, celery, and garlic to now-empty pot and cook until softened, 3 to 5 minutes.

**2**   Add wine, scraping up any browned bits, then add beef and any accumulated juices, potatoes, carrots, broth, and Worcestershire. Lock lid in place and close pressure-release valve. Select high pressure-cook function and cook for 50 minutes.

**3**   Turn off Instant Pot and quick-release pressure. Carefully remove lid, allowing steam to escape away from you. Transfer roast to carving board, tent with aluminum foil, and let rest for 15 to 20 minutes. Transfer vegetables to serving dish and tent with foil. Using large spoon, skim fat from surface of sauce.

**4**   Slice meat against grain ½ inch thick and arrange on serving dish with vegetables. Serve, passing sauce separately.

## Antoinette's Tips

Use potatoes measuring 2½ to 3 inches in diameter.

You can use whole baby carrots, if you've got them, instead of prepping regular carrots.

# Instant Pot Beef Ragu

**Serves:** 8 to 12 (makes 8 cups; enough for 2 pounds pasta)   •   **Total time:** 1¾ hours

*Budget-friendly beef chuck eye becomes incredibly tender and flavorful when cooked under pressure. Here you add a host of pantry-friendly ingredients to create an aromatic sauce that will make your taste buds very happy. The best part? The Instant Pot infuses the meat with mouthwatering flavors in a fraction of the time it would take to simmer a ragu on the stovetop. So, whether you're hosting a dinner party and want to serve this over fresh pasta or you want to treat yourself to a cozy night in and simply scoop this up with crusty bread, this incredible ragu will leave you feeling like a culinary superstar. Bon appétit, boo!*

2   carrots, peeled and cut into ½-inch pieces

2   shallots, cut into ½-inch pieces

2   celery ribs, cut into ½-inch pieces

1½  pounds boneless beef chuck-eye roast, trimmed and cut into 3 pieces

1   teaspoon table salt

½   teaspoon pepper

1   tablespoon extra-virgin olive oil

2   garlic cloves, minced

1   teaspoon tomato paste

1   teaspoon minced fresh thyme

½   teaspoon garlic powder

1   (28-ounce) can fire-roasted crushed tomatoes

1½  cups beef broth

¼   cup red wine

1   bay leaf

1   ounce Parmesan cheese, grated (½ cup)

**1**   Pulse carrots, shallots, and celery in food processor until finely chopped, 8 to 10 pulses. Pat beef dry with paper towels and sprinkle with salt and pepper. Using highest sauté function, heat oil in Instant Pot until just smoking. Add beef and cook until well browned on all sides, 7 to 10 minutes. Transfer to large plate. Add vegetable mixture to fat left in pot and cook until beginning to brown, 3 to 5 minutes.

**2**   Stir in garlic, tomato paste, thyme, and garlic powder and cook until fragrant, about 1 minute. Stir in tomatoes, broth, wine, and bay leaf. Return beef and any accumulated juices to pot. Lock lid into place and close pressure-release valve. Select high pressure-cook function and cook for 1 hour.

**3**   Turn off Instant Pot and quick-release pressure. Carefully remove lid, allowing steam to escape away from you. Remove and discard bay leaf. Transfer meat to cutting board and let cool slightly. Shred meat into bite-size pieces, then return to pot along with any accumulated juices. Stir in Parmesan and season with salt and pepper to taste. (Sauce can be refrigerated for up to 2 days or frozen for up to 1 month.)

## *Pantry Pick*

**Fire-roasted tomatoes:** I reach for fire-roasted tomatoes when I'm looking for an easy way to add a subtly caramelized, slightly smoky tomato flavor. They make dishes like this ragu taste like they've cooked for longer than they really have.

# Instant Pot Quesabirria Tacos

**Serves:** 4 · **Total time:** 2½ hours

*Birria tacos have become superpopular in recent years, with good reason. To make these messy, fun-to-eat tacos, meat (often goat in Mexico, but usually beef in the United States) is braised until tender with chiles, garlic, herbs, spices, and other ingredients. The meat is shredded for the filling, the assembled tacos are griddled to crisp them up, and the braising broth is served alongside for dipping the tacos. Quesabirria tacos introduce cheese for even more fabulousness. Inspired by the popularity of this iconic street food, I've created a recipe that brings the excitement home. Dried chiles bring complexity to the pressure-cooked beef filling. The tender meat, flavorful spices, and a burst of fresh toppings come together to create a quesabirria taco experience that's nothing short of extraordinary.*

## Birria

- 1 tomato, cored
- 1 shallot, peeled
- 1 garlic clove, peeled
- 3 dried New Mexican chiles, stemmed and seeded
- ½ teaspoon red pepper flakes
- 1½ cups beef broth, divided
- 1½ teaspoons table salt, divided
- ½ teaspoon ground cumin
- ¼ teaspoon garlic powder
- ⅛ teaspoon ground cloves
- 1½ pounds boneless beef chuck-eye roast, trimmed and cut into 3 pieces
- 1 teaspoon extra-virgin olive oil
- 1 teaspoon apple cider vinegar

## Tacos

- 12 (6-inch) corn tortillas
- 4 ounces Monterey Jack cheese, shredded (1 cup)
- ¼ cup finely chopped white onion
- ¼ cup minced fresh cilantro
- Lime wedges

**1** For the birria: Using highest sauté function, cook tomato, shallot, and garlic in Instant Pot until charred all over, about 15 minutes. Add chiles and pepper flakes and toast for 5 minutes, stirring frequently. Add 1 cup broth and ½ teaspoon salt and cook until chiles are softened, 5 to 7 minutes. Transfer to blender and process until smooth, 30 seconds to 1 minute. Wipe pot clean with paper towels.

**2** Combine cumin, garlic powder, cloves, and remaining 1 teaspoon salt in small bowl. Pat beef dry with paper towels, then sprinkle evenly with salt mixture. Using highest sauté function, heat oil in now-empty pot until just smoking, about 5 minutes. Add beef to pot and cook until well browned all over, about 12 minutes. Add reserved chile mixture along with vinegar and remaining ½ cup broth. Lock lid in place and close pressure-release valve. Select high pressure-cook function and cook for 1 hour.

**3** Turn off Instant Pot and quick-release pressure. Carefully remove lid, allowing steam to escape away from you. Using tongs or slotted spoon, transfer meat to large bowl, then use 2 forks to shred meat fine. Reserve sauce in pot.

## *Pantry Pick*

**New Mexican chiles:** These relatively mild dried chiles pack a warm, earthy punch. Purchase dried chiles that feel pliable and not overly dry—you want them to bend without cracking. Then, just remove the stem and seeds before using them.

**4**    For the tacos: Adjust oven rack to middle position and heat oven to 200 degrees. Set wire rack in rimmed baking sheet and line with triple layer of paper towels. Drag 1 side of 3 tortillas through sauce in pot and place tortillas in 12-inch nonstick skillet, sauced side down (tortillas will overlap slightly). Top each tortilla evenly with 2 tablespoons cheese, then spread scant ¼ cup birria meat over half of each tortilla. Cook over medium heat until most of cheese has melted, 2 to 3 minutes.

**5**    Sprinkle 1 teaspoon onion and 1 teaspoon cilantro over meat, then fold nonmeat half of tortilla over meat using spatula and tongs. Cook tacos until crisp on both sides, 1 to 2 minutes per side. Transfer tacos to prepared rack and place in oven to keep warm. Wipe skillet clean with paper towels and repeat with remaining tortillas, sauce, cheese, meat, onion, and cilantro. Portion reserved sauce into individual serving bowls. Serve tacos with lime wedges and sauce.

## *Antoinette's Tips*

You can substitute dried guajillo chiles for the New Mexican chiles.

When assembling the tacos in steps 4 and 5, your skillet will be hotter for subsequent batches, so the tacos may crisp up faster.

# Instant Pot Barbecue Ribs

**Serves:** 4 · **Total time:** 1¼ hours

*Alright, y'all, get ready to level up your rib game with these finger-lickin'-good baby back ribs. We all know that making ribs can be a labor of love, but with the help of the trusty Instant Pot, I've created a version that makes them a whole lot easier and faster while being just as delicious as any cooked outside. This recipe uses the same pressure-cooking and broiling technique that I use for my Instant Pot Barbecue Burnt Ends (page 125), which results in tender, fall-off-the-bone ribs with a crispy crust. When it comes to preparing pork ribs for cooking, a little prep work goes a long way in ensuring tender and flavorful results. Start by removing the thin translucent membrane on the back of the ribs, as it can prevent the flavors of the seasoning from penetrating the meat. Then, generously season the ribs with dry rub and pop them into the pot with some of the sauce. The rest of the sauce gets slathered on after broiling.*

| | |
|---|---|
| 1 | (3-pound) rack baby back ribs, trimmed and membrane removed |
| 7 | teaspoons Barbecue Spice Rub (page 55), divided |
| 1 | tablespoon vegetable oil |
| 1½ | cups water |
| 1½ | cups Barbecue Sauce (page 54), divided |

**1** Cut between rib bones using chef's knife to divide rib rack into 4 equal pieces. Pat ribs dry with paper towels, then rub 5 teaspoons spice rub all over ribs. Using highest sauté function, heat oil in Instant Pot until just smoking. Add half of ribs, meat side down, and cook until well browned on 1 side, 5 to 7 minutes. Transfer to large plate and repeat with remaining ribs.

**2** Add water and 1 cup barbecue sauce to now-empty pot, then nestle browned ribs and any accumulated juices into sauce, stacking ribs as needed. Lock lid into place and close pressure-release valve. Select high pressure-cook function and cook for 45 minutes.

**3** Adjust oven rack 6 inches from boiler element and heat broiler. Line rimmed baking sheet with aluminum foil. Combine remaining ½ cup barbecue sauce and remaining 2 teaspoons spice rub in bowl. Turn off Instant Pot and quick-release pressure. Carefully remove lid, allowing steam to escape away from you. Transfer ribs to prepared sheet, meat side up, and broil until well browned, 5 to 7 minutes. Brush ribs with reserved barbecue sauce mixture and let rest for 5 minutes. Serve.

## Antoinette's Tips

Use a paring knife to cut slits in the membrane, and then use your fingers to pull it away from the ribs.

I definitely recommend using both the homemade spice rub and the homemade sauce, because the flavors work so well together and that's all the seasoning these ribs get. In a pinch, you could substitute store-bought, but the finished flavors will be quite different.

## Antoinette's Tip

Pork butt roast, often labeled Boston butt in the supermarket, actually comes from the shoulder. Its high level of connective tissue and marbling make it ideal for transforming into barbecued pulled pork.

# Instant Pot Carolina-Style Pulled Pork

**Serves:** 8 · **Total time:** 1¼ hours, plus 30 minutes resting

*Let me tell you, attempting to get my grandpa's secret recipe for pulled pork was like trying to crack a vault. I had to use all my charm and persuasion to get him to spill the beans—and I'm not sure I got the whole story! This version of his famous recipe is as close as it's going to get, but I promise you won't be disappointed. Eastern Carolina barbecue sauce is a vinegar-based sauce with a tangy and sharp flavor profile. Here the sauce is the flavorful liquid left in the pot after cooking the pork. The acidic properties of the apple cider vinegar help break down the connective tissues in the pork butt, resulting in a more tender and juicy texture. When you go for seconds, don't thank me—thank my grandpa. Serve this on buns or on its own, with coleslaw, potato salad, collard greens, corn—any of your favorite barbecue sides.*

¼ cup seasoned salt, divided

1½ tablespoons garlic powder

1 tablespoon unseasoned meat tenderizer

1 (4-pound) boneless pork butt roast, trimmed and quartered

1 cup apple cider vinegar

1 cup water

¼ cup packed dark brown sugar

1½ teaspoons liquid smoke

1½ teaspoons red pepper flakes

**1** Combine seasoned salt, garlic powder, and meat tenderizer in bowl. Rub pork all over with salt mixture. Let sit for 30 minutes.

**2** Combine vinegar, water, sugar, liquid smoke, and pepper flakes in Instant Pot, whisking to dissolve sugar. Add pork, then lock lid into place and close pressure-release valve. Select high pressure-cook function and cook for 45 minutes.

**3** Turn off Instant Pot and quick-release pressure. Carefully remove lid, allowing steam to escape away from you. Transfer pork to cutting board and let rest until cool enough to handle, about 10 minutes. Pull pork into large chunks, then chop or shred into bite-size pieces.

**4** Whisk cooking liquid to recombine, then pour into serving bowl and serve with chopped pork to taste.

## *Pantry Pick*

**Seasoned salt:** This one-stop blend of salt, herbs, spices, and sometimes sugar adds multidimensional flavor to meat, potatoes, corn, and more. I usually use Lawry's Seasoned Salt.

# Instant Pot Cajun-Inspired Shrimp and Rice

**Serves:** 4 · **Total time:** 1 hour

*Savor the flavors of the bayou with this one-pot wonder that practically cooks itself. Traditional recipes for Cajun shrimp and rice are true cultural and culinary gems, but my simplified version still captures the robust, rustic spirit of Cajun cuisine. It combines tender, sweet shrimp, perfectly cooked rice, and a symphony of spices (plus the Cajun "trinity" of onion, bell pepper, and celery) that will take you on a food journey to Louisiana. It's a supremely satisfying one-dish meal made nearly effortless through the convenience of the Instant Pot.*

| | |
|---|---|
| 1 | tablespoon extra-virgin olive oil |
| 1 | onion, chopped fine |
| 1 | small green bell pepper, stemmed, seeded, and cut into ¼-inch pieces |
| 2 | celery ribs, minced |
| 1¼ | teaspoons table salt, divided |
| ½ | teaspoon pepper, divided |
| 2 | teaspoons garlic powder, divided |
| 1 | teaspoon Old Bay seasoning, divided |
| 2 | cups beef broth |
| 1 | tablespoon Texas Pete Hot Sauce |
| 1 | bay leaf |
| 1½ | cups long-grain white rice, rinsed and drained |
| 1 | pound extra-large shrimp (21 to 25 per pound), peeled, deveined, and tails removed |

**1** Using highest sauté function, heat oil in Instant Pot until shimmering. Add onion, bell pepper, celery, 1 teaspoon salt, and ¼ teaspoon pepper and cook until vegetables are softened, 5 to 7 minutes.

**2** Add 1 teaspoon garlic powder and ½ teaspoon Old Bay and cook, stirring frequently, until fragrant, about 30 seconds. Stir in broth, hot sauce, and bay leaf, scraping up any browned bits, then stir in rice. Lock lid into place and close pressure-release valve. Select high pressure-cook function and cook for 25 minutes.

**3** Pat shrimp dry with paper towels, then toss with remaining ¼ teaspoon salt, remaining ¼ teaspoon pepper, remaining 1 teaspoon garlic powder, and remaining ½ teaspoon Old Bay. Turn off Instant Pot and quick-release pressure. Carefully remove lid, allowing steam to escape away from you. Discard bay leaf and stir in shrimp. Partially cover pot and let sit until shrimp are opaque, 5 to 8 minutes. Serve.

## *Pantry Pick*

**Shrimp:** Unless you have access to fresh-caught shrimp (lucky you if you do), that "fresh" shrimp at the fish counter has probably been previously frozen. Most commercial shrimp is flash-frozen right on the boat, so for the best quality, you're better off buying bagged frozen shrimp to stock your freezer. (The machine used to shell shrimp beats up the delicate shrimp, so shell-on is better.) An added bonus is that bagged frozen shrimp is often less expensive than fresh.

### Antoinette's Tip

Rinsing the rice before adding it to the Instant Pot makes for a better texture in the finished dish, because rinsing removes excess surface starch that would otherwise make the cooked grains clump together and turn sticky.

# Instant Pot Collard Greens

**Serves:** 6 to 8 · **Total time:** 1¾ hours

*Collard greens cooked long and slow with smoked or cured meat until tender and highly seasoned with plenty of "pot likker" is classic Southern soul food cooking. The meat is often turkey wings or necks, or ham hocks or pork feet, and the greens are often spicy with some kind of red pepper. (And yes, I like mine spicy.) Now, I know what you're thinking: "Didn't she already share a recipe for collard greens?" Well, yes, but this one is quite different. While the Weeknight Collard Greens on page 35 use canned collards and are perfect for hectic weeknights, this one stays closer to the classic long-cooked version using fresh greens, while speeding things up with the Instant Pot. The cooking time may be on the long side, but it's totally hands-off and is still faster than making this preparation on the stovetop—and you'll still end up with silky, soul-soothing collards infused with mouth-awakening Southern flavors.*

| | |
|---|---|
| 2 | pounds collard greens, stems trimmed |
| 1 | tablespoon extra-virgin olive oil |
| 1 | onion, chopped fine |
| 1 | teaspoon table salt |
| ½ | teaspoon pepper |
| 1 | pound smoked turkey wings |
| 2 | cups beef broth |
| 1 | cup water |
| 4 | garlic cloves, minced |
| 1 | tablespoon apple cider vinegar |
| 1 | tablespoon packed dark brown sugar |
| 1 | teaspoon seasoned salt |
| ½ | teaspoon cayenne pepper |

**1** Cut collards into thirds lengthwise. Stack slices and cut crosswise 1 inch thick. Using highest sauté function, heat oil in Instant Pot until shimmering. Add onion, salt, and pepper and cook until softened, about 5 minutes. Stir in collards in 2 batches, waiting until first batch is wilted to add second batch. Stir in turkey wings, broth, water, garlic, vinegar, sugar, seasoned salt, and cayenne. Lock lid in place and close pressure-release valve. Select high pressure-cook function and cook for 1 hour.

**2** Turn off Instant Pot and quick-release pressure. Carefully remove lid, allowing steam to escape away from you. Transfer turkey wings to cutting board (wings will be very tender, so be sure to pick through collards for any loose bones) and let cool for 10 minutes. Remove meat from turkey wings and return to pot; discard skin and bones. Season collards with salt to taste, and serve.

## *Pantry Pick*

**Smoked turkey wings:** If you haven't had smoked turkey wings before, you're in for a delicious treat. They freeze well, so they're easy to keep on hand for adding a smoky-meaty accent to dishes like these collards. Turkey wings are obviously a lot larger than chicken wings, so don't be surprised if one wing makes up the pound! You can substitute an equal weight of smoked turkey necks for the wings, if desired.

# Chapter 5

# Oven and Done

Oven-Roasted Smothered Chicken Thighs

Royce's Mini Chicken

Not Your Mother's Meatloaf

Thyme-Mustard Crusted Pork Chops

Oven-Roasted Lemon and Dill Branzino

No-Boil Mushroom and Pea Penne

Bacon–Green Chile Quiche

Mini Carbonara Quiche Cups

Dijon-Lemon Roasted Cabbage Wedges

# Oven-Roasted Smothered Chicken Thighs

**Serves:** 2 to 4 · **Total time:** 1 hour

*Prepare yourself for a Southern-style feast that'll make your taste buds dance with joy: smothered chicken thighs enveloped in luscious gravy, without the hassle of being tied to the kitchen. The usual method for making smothered chicken is to cook it on the stovetop, first partially cooking the chicken by itself and then removing it from the skillet, making a gravy, and then placing the chicken back in the pan so it can finish cooking as the sauce thickens. This produces moist pieces of chicken in a flavorful, velvety gravy, but it's pretty hands-on. My revamped recipe delivers the same irresistible experience without the sweat. You simply put your ingredients in a baking pan, place the pan in the oven, and with a simple whisk at the end, you have tender and delicious smothered chicken. It's nice to serve this with something to soak up every drop of the gravy, like rice, potatoes, or crusty bread.*

| | |
|---|---|
| 1½ | teaspoons onion powder |
| 1½ | teaspoons garlic powder |
| 1 | teaspoon table salt |
| ¾ | teaspoon smoked paprika |
| ¾ | teaspoon pepper |
| ½ | cup beef broth |
| 2 | tablespoons all-purpose flour |
| 2 | tablespoons Worcestershire sauce |
| 4 | (5- to 7-ounce) bone-in chicken thighs, trimmed |
| 2 | ounces cremini mushrooms, trimmed and sliced ¼ inch thick |
| ½ | cup thinly sliced onion |
| ¼ | cup chopped celery |

**1**  Adjust oven rack to middle position and heat oven to 400 degrees. Combine onion powder, garlic powder, salt, paprika, and pepper in bowl. In separate bowl, whisk broth, flour, and Worcestershire until combined.

**2**  Pat chicken dry with paper towels, then rub all over with spice mixture, being sure to rub mixture under skin. Scatter mushrooms, onion, and celery over bottom of 8-inch square baking pan. Pour broth mixture over top, then nestle chicken thighs into sauce. Cover pan tightly with aluminum foil and bake until chicken registers at least 195 degrees, about 45 minutes.

**3**  Transfer chicken to serving platter and whisk vegetables and sauce left in pan to recombine. Pour sauce and vegetables over chicken. Serve.

## *Pantry Pick*

**Smoked paprika:** I've mentioned before how appealing I find a smoky element in a dish, and this spice infuses smoky, woodsy, slightly fruity complexity into anything you add it to. It's natural, too—the dried red peppers are smoked over wood fires before being ground.

## Antoinette's Tip

You can purchase presliced cremini mushrooms to speed up prep.

# Royce's Mini Chicken

**Serves:** 1 · **Total time:** 1¼ hours

*During our kitchen adventures, my imaginative young daughter, Royce, refers to Cornish hens as "mini chickens." She loves helping me in the kitchen and requests that I make this dish for dinner at least once a week. Whenever I do, I always buy two Cornish hens so that we can each season our own to taste. While I'm grabbing the lemon and garlic, Royce is going straight for my homemade barbecue rub to spice up her personal chicken like a true culinary diva. The rub is sweet and smoky, with a kick that creeps out right at the end. Combining the seasoning with butter and rubbing it under and on top of the skin before roasting the whole hen on a rack results in meat that is juicy and skin that is crisp, with both seasoned just right. This recipe is written for one Cornish game hen to serve one person, but it can be easily scaled to serve up to four people with four hens.*

3   tablespoons unsalted butter, melted

3   tablespoons Barbecue Spice Rub
    (page 55)

1   (1½-pound) Cornish hen, giblets
    discarded

**1**   Adjust oven rack to middle position and heat oven to 400 degrees. Set wire rack in aluminum foil–lined rimmed baking sheet and spray rack with vegetable oil spray. Combine melted butter and spice rub in bowl.

**2**   Pat hen dry with paper towels. Using your fingers, gently loosen skin covering breast and thighs. Rub half of butter mixture under skin, directly on meat in center of each side of breast and on thighs. Gently press on skin to distribute butter mixture over meat. Brush remaining butter mixture all over skin. Transfer hen to prepared rack.

**3**   Roast hen until breast registers 160 degrees, 45 minutes to 1 hour. Transfer to large plate and let rest for 10 minutes. Serve.

## Antoinette's Tip

Making a sort of paste with the melted butter and spice rub makes it easy to distribute this seasoning evenly both under and on top of the hen's skin, so that every bite is infused with flavor.

### Antoinette's Tip

Make sure not to over-knead the beef mixture in step 2. Doing so will lead to a meatloaf that is dense and tough rather than tender and juicy.

# Not Your Mother's Meatloaf

**Serves:** 2 to 4  ·  **Total time:** 1 hour

*This is not the typical humdrum meatloaf that you might remember with a grimace from childhood. For starters, there's no questionable ketchup-heavy topping. And rather than using onion in the meat mix, I up the ante with minced shallot. Blending in Marsala and Pecorino Romano cheese along with the traditional Worcestershire sauce builds rich, complex flavors. Then, instead of packing everything into a loaf pan, I take advantage of a test kitchen innovation by shaping the loaf and baking it on a wire rack set on a baking sheet. This drains away excess fat, so you won't be left with a dense, gelatinous loaf of meat. With a sweet and savory store-bought onion jam slathered on before it goes into the oven, this meatloaf turns out juicy and delicious. Are you ready to indulge in this elevated meatloaf makeover?*

| | |
|---|---|
| 2 | large eggs |
| ¼ | cup panko bread crumbs |
| ¼ | cup finely grated Pecorino Romano cheese |
| 2 | tablespoons dry Marsala |
| 1 | shallot, minced |
| 1 | tablespoon Worcestershire sauce |
| 1 | teaspoon Italian seasoning |
| ¾ | teaspoon table salt |
| ½ | teaspoon pepper |
| 1 | pound 80 percent lean ground beef |
| ¼ | cup caramelized onion jam |

**1**  Adjust oven rack to upper-middle position and heat oven to 400 degrees. Set wire rack in aluminum foil–lined rimmed baking sheet. Fold piece of heavy-duty foil into 10 by 6-inch rectangle, lay on half of rack, then poke holes in foil with skewer about every ½ inch. Spray rack and foil with vegetable oil spray.

**2**  Combine eggs, panko, Pecorino, Marsala, shallot, Worcestershire, Italian seasoning, salt, and pepper in large bowl. Add beef and knead with your hands until well combined. Transfer meat mixture to foil rectangle on prepared sheet and shape into 9 by 5-inch meatloaf. Spread onion jam evenly over top and sides.

**3**  Bake until meatloaf registers 160 degrees, 40 to 50 minutes. Transfer meatloaf to cutting board and let rest for 5 minutes. Slice meatloaf and serve.

## *Pantry Pick*

**Caramelized onion jam:** This sweet-savory condiment is often used on cheese plates or sandwiches, but I incorporate it into my cooking too. There are many good jarred onion jams on grocery shelves; I usually buy whatever is on sale.

# Thyme-Mustard Crusted Pork Chops

**Serves:** 4 · **Total time:** 35 minutes

*By this point in the book, it should be clear that mustard is my favorite condiment to cook with. It comes in so many varieties—each type brings something a little different to a dish, but all offer so much flavor. Here I use stone-ground mustard (also called coarse-ground mustard), which has a bit of heat and rustic, grainy texture, since the mustard seeds are not completely ground. When paired with salty, nutty Pecorino Romano cheese and some fresh thyme, it makes an amazing coating for neutral-tasting pork chops for a dish that tastes like far more than the sum of its parts. Making slashes in the chops before slathering the mixture over them allows all those flavors to penetrate deep into the meat. If you're tired of dry and boring chops, you'll definitely want to keep this recipe in your rotation.*

4   (10- to 15-ounce) bone-in pork rib or center-cut chops, 1 to 1¼ inches thick, trimmed

2   teaspoons table salt

1   teaspoon pepper

¼   cup stone-ground mustard

3   tablespoons grated Pecorino Romano cheese

2   teaspoons chopped fresh thyme

**1**   Adjust oven rack 6 inches from broiler element and heat oven to 400 degrees. Set wire rack in aluminum foil–lined rimmed baking sheet and spray with vegetable oil spray. Pat chops dry with paper towels; then, using paring knife, stab chops every ½ inch, making sure to penetrate meat completely. Go back and make a second cut perpendicular to each initial cut, creating an "x." Sprinkle salt and pepper evenly over both sides of chops, then transfer to prepared rack.

**2**   Combine mustard, Pecorino, and thyme in bowl, then spread mixture evenly over both sides of chops. Transfer to oven and bake until pork registers 115 to 120 degrees, 12 to 15 minutes.

**3**   Heat broiler element and broil until chops register 135 to 140 degrees, 5 to 7 minutes. Let chops rest for 5 minutes. Serve.

## *Pantry Pick*

**Stone-ground mustard:** Many mustards are made by finely grinding the seeds, but stone-ground or coarse-ground mustard contains seeds that are only partially ground (or left whole). That textural contrast works great in this recipe where the mustard plays a starring role. The test kitchen's favorite is Grey Poupon Harvest Coarse Ground Mustard.

### Antoinette's Tip

Broilers can vary dramatically across brands and models, so I recommend paying attention to the temperature of the pork rather than the level of browning to determine doneness in step 3.

## Antoinette's Tips

When you're buying whole fish, keep in mind that it should never smell fishy. The eyes should be clear and shiny and the fish should feel firm, not soft or mushy.

If your market doesn't have whole branzino, try whole black sea bass or red snapper instead.

# Oven-Roasted Lemon and Dill Branzino

**Serves:** 1 · **Total time:** 35 minutes

*Cooking a whole fish might seem intimidating, but I promise you that it's a lot easier than you think. No need for fancy knife skills or fishy business here. A lot of people think you have to be a master butcher to prep fish for cooking, but that is not the case. When you're buying fresh whole fish, simply tell the fishmonger how you plan on preparing the fish, and they will take care of scaling, gutting, and gilling the fish for you, as needed. Now let's talk about branzino. It's sized just right for one person and is a delicate fish with a mild, almost sweet flavor, which pairs beautifully here with lemon and dill. This is a fantastic recipe to break out when company comes over, since it is easily scaled up as needed, it can be made quickly and is failproof, and it's most definitely a show-stopping dish.*

1 (1-pound) whole branzino, scaled, gutted, and fins snipped off with scissors

1 teaspoon extra-virgin olive oil

1 teaspoon table salt

½ teaspoon pepper

¼ teaspoon grated lemon zest plus 2 (¼-inch-thick) lemon slices, halved crosswise

4 sprigs fresh dill

**1** Adjust oven rack to middle position and heat oven to 450 degrees. Line rimmed baking sheet with aluminum foil and spray with vegetable oil spray. Rinse branzino under cold running water and pat dry with paper towels inside and out. Place branzino on prepared sheet and rub all over with oil. Sprinkle inside and out with salt and pepper. Stuff cavity with lemon slices and dill sprigs, then sprinkle lemon zest over top of fish.

**2** Roast until branzino flakes apart when gently prodded with paring knife and registers 140 degrees, 10 to 12 minutes.

**3** Carefully transfer branzino to cutting board and let rest for 5 minutes. Fillet branzino by making vertical cut just behind head from top of fish to belly; discard lemon slices and dill sprigs. Make another cut along top of branzino from head to tail. Use spatula to lift meat from bones, starting at head end and running spatula over bones to lift out fillet. Repeat on other side of branzino. Discard head and skeleton. Serve.

# No-Boil Mushroom and Pea Penne

**Serves:** 2 or 3 · **Total time:** 1¼ hours

*Let's talk wine. I am no sommelier, but I love to cook with wine: It's an easy way to add flavor complexity and instantly upgrade a dish. One of my goals with this book is to encourage you at home to buy and use ingredients that might be outside your comfort zone—to venture down uncharted grocery aisles and get comfortable with experimenting in the kitchen. I did these things myself when learning to cook with Marsala. Though I was familiar with chicken Marsala, I wanted to showcase the power of this ingredient in a way that did not include meat. This simple recipe involves pouring all the ingredients into a pan and sliding that pan into the oven. What emerges is perfectly cooked pasta in a cream sauce that is entangled with nutty flavor. It comes out of the oven slightly soupy but thickens as it sits. It's very rich, so I often serve small portions alongside a big green salad. Since Marsala is fortified, you can refrigerate leftovers for a few months. I bet you'll use it all up making this dish before then, though. (For another way to use Marsala, see Not Your Mother's Meatloaf on page 147.)*

| | |
|---|---|
| 2¼ | cups heavy cream |
| 8 | ounces penne |
| 4 | ounces cremini mushrooms, trimmed and sliced thin |
| ½ | cup frozen peas |
| 1 | cup chicken broth |
| 1 | ounce Pecorino Romano cheese, finely grated (½ cup) |
| 6 | tablespoons dry Marsala |
| 1 | teaspoon table salt |
| ½ | teaspoon garlic powder |
| ½ | teaspoon onion powder |
| ½ | teaspoon pepper |

**1** Adjust oven rack to middle position and heat oven to 400 degrees. Add all ingredients to 8-inch square baking pan, stirring to combine and ensuring most of noodles are submerged. Cover pan tightly with aluminum foil, place on aluminum foil–lined rimmed baking sheet, and bake until pasta is tender, 45 minutes to 1 hour.

**2** Remove foil from pan and stir to combine. Let sit for 10 minutes before serving.

## *Pantry Pick*

**Marsala:** This Italian fortified wine is available in sweet and dry styles. I reach for the dry style when I'm cooking. Don't buy anything labeled "Marsala cooking wine," since that contains salt and other unnecessary additives.

## Antoinette's Tips

I used Barilla brand penne when developing this recipe. If you use a different brand, you may need to check for doneness earlier. I do recommend penne because it packs tightly into the baking dish, helping ensure that all the pieces are submerged and cook evenly.

You can purchase presliced cremini mushrooms to speed up prep.

# Bacon–Green Chile Quiche

**Serves:** 6 · **Total time:** 1½ hours, plus 1 hour chilling and cooling

*The versatility of this dish makes it perfect for a light dinner, breakfast, or brunch; it can be served with a simple green salad for dinner, fruit salad for breakfast, or as part of a larger brunch spread. You might think that quiche is a bit of a culinary challenge to master, but using store-bought pie dough makes this totally achievable. After nestling the dough round into the pie plate, chilling it for a bit, and parbaking it on its own, you then just mix up your eggy filling, pour it in, and bake. I prefer sharp cheddar cheese, since it provides extra flavor that pairs well with the smoky bacon and tangy green chiles. You can substitute fully cooked bacon and skip having to cook the bacon in step 2. You can use a frozen, preshaped pie crust if you prefer; just make sure to use a deep-dish crust or you may not be able to fit all the egg mixture in the crust. If you use a frozen preshaped pie crust, skip step 1 and parbake the crust from frozen as directed in step 4.*

1 (9-inch) store-bought pie dough round, room temperature

6 slices bacon, sliced ½ inch thick

1¼ cups heavy cream, divided

1 tablespoon cornstarch

5 large eggs

¼ teaspoon table salt

½ cup canned chopped green chiles

4 ounces sharp cheddar cheese, shredded (1 cup)

**1** Unroll pie dough round and center dough over 9-inch pie plate. Ease dough into pie plate by gently lifting edge of dough with your hand while pressing into plate bottom and sides with your other hand. Crimp dough by evenly pressing fork tines into dough on lip of plate. Trim any excess dough that hangs over edge of plate. Wrap dough-lined plate loosely in plastic wrap and refrigerate until firm, about 30 minutes.

**2** While dough chills, cook bacon in 12-inch nonstick skillet over medium heat until crispy, 8 to 10 minutes. Using slotted spoon, transfer bacon to paper towel–lined plate and set aside. Adjust oven rack to middle position and heat oven to 350 degrees.

**3** Whisk ¼ cup cream and cornstarch in large bowl until cornstarch dissolves. Whisk in eggs, salt, and remaining 1 cup cream until mixture is smooth; set aside.

## Pantry Picks

### Store-bought pie dough:
The convenience of being able to use store-bought pie crust on any given night far outweighs the slight drop in quality from homemade. Once you taste this quiche, I think you'll agree. The test kitchen's favorite store-bought dough is Pillsbury Refrigerated Pie Crusts.

### Canned green chiles:
These tiny taste grenades explode with flavor wherever they're deployed, plus they're available in small cans that are very easy to use up. The test kitchen's pick is Goya Diced Green Chiles Fire Roasted.

**4** Line chilled pie shell with double layer of parchment paper and fill with pie weights. Bake on rimmed baking sheet for 15 minutes. Remove parchment and weights; rotate plate; and bake until bottom dries out and turns light golden brown, about 10 minutes.

**5** Whisk filling to recombine. With pie still on sheet, sprinkle reserved bacon, chiles, and cheese in bottom of warm pie crust. Gently pour cream mixture over top and bake until toothpick inserted in center of quiche comes out clean and center registers 170 degrees, about 40 minutes, covering crust with aluminum foil during baking if crust begins to get too dark. Transfer to wire rack and let cool for 30 minutes. Serve warm or at room temperature.

### Antoinette's Tip

Letting the pie dough come to room temperature helps with unrolling the dough out of the packaging, making it less likely to tear.

# Mini Carbonara Quiche Cups

**Serves:** 6 as an appetizer or 2 as a main · **Total time:** 20 minutes

*Ever wonder what happens when a flavor craving meets leftover ingredients? Enter the world of my Mini Carbonara Quiche Cups. Although eggs are known to be one of the "big three" of a grocery list (milk, bread, and eggs), I don't cook with eggs on a regular basis, so I don't buy them unless I'm making a specific dish. This recipe is a direct result of me craving my favorite version of pasta carbonara one night, making it, and then figuring out what to do with the leftover ingredients—eggs, prosciutto, and cream—before they went bad. The shell is a crispy, salty piece of baked prosciutto that's filled with a fluffy egg-and-potato mixture, accompanied by tangy pecorino cheese and grated black pepper. The shredded potatoes are obviously a departure from pasta, but they go so well with the prosciutto and eggs—it's a whole new way to look at carbonara! Break out this spin on traditional pastry quiche cups to host a brunch that'll leave your guests in awe. Use the large holes of a box grater to shred the potatoes. This recipe can easily be doubled and made in a 12-cup muffin tin.*

6   thin slices prosciutto (3 ounces)

2   large eggs

1   small russet potato, peeled and shredded (½ cup)

¼   cup heavy cream

¼   cup finely grated Pecorino Romano cheese

1   teaspoon pepper

**1**   Adjust oven rack to middle position and heat oven to 375 degrees. Spray 6-cup muffin tin with vegetable oil spray, then line bottom and sides with 1 slice prosciutto each, folding and cutting prosciutto as needed.

**2**   Whisk eggs, potato, cream, Pecorino, and pepper together in bowl. Divide egg mixture evenly among prepared muffin cups and bake until eggs are set and paring knife inserted into center comes out clean, 15 to 20 minutes.

**3**   Let cool for 5 minutes, then remove from muffin tin and serve.

## *Pantry Pick*

**Prosciutto:** It wasn't that many years ago that the only way to buy prosciutto was to pay a premium at an Italian market. Nowadays there are many good-quality North American–produced prosciuttos that bring this silky, porky goodness within everyday reach. If you're buying presliced prosciutto, make sure it's thinly sliced.

## Antoinette's Tip

Make sure you leave the core intact when cutting the cabbage into wedges. This ensures that the wedges stay together and brown evenly while roasting.

# Dijon-Lemon Roasted Cabbage Wedges

**Serves:** 4 · **Total time:** 45 minutes

*There are two recipes in this cookbook that changed my life forever, and here's one of them (the other one is my Instant Pot Barbecue Burnt Ends recipe on page 125). Fans of America's Test Kitchen: The Next Generation know that I made a version of this dish for my final challenge on the show. We were tasked with creating two recipes that we would want to include in our cookbook if we won the competition, and not only did we have to make these dishes, but our dishes also had to represent two different chapters in our cookbook. Though this recipe's shining moment was when it led me to victory, I'll never forget its origins, on the night of March 14, 2021. I stayed up until 2 a.m. cooking and recording a full recipe run-through. It wasn't for a sponsorship, I didn't do this for work, there was no immediate benefit to come—I was just having fun turning humble ingredients into tender delicacies. By brushing cabbage wedges with a flavorful sauce of Dijon mustard, lemon juice, oil, garlic, and red pepper flakes, you, too, can transform an inexpensive, "boring" vegetable into something spectacular.*

1 head green cabbage (2 pounds)
3 tablespoons Dijon mustard
3 tablespoons lemon juice
2 tablespoons extra-virgin olive oil
3 garlic cloves, minced
1 teaspoon table salt
½ teaspoon pepper
¼ teaspoon red pepper flakes
2 tablespoons chopped fresh parsley

**1** Adjust oven rack to lowest position and heat oven to 500 degrees. Halve cabbage through core and cut each half into 4 approximately 2-inch-wide wedges, leaving core intact (you will have 8 wedges).

**2** Spray aluminum foil–lined rimmed baking sheet with vegetable oil spray. Arrange wedges in single layer on prepared sheet. Whisk mustard, lemon juice, oil, garlic, salt, pepper, and pepper flakes together in bowl. Measure out and reserve 3 tablespoons mustard mixture, then brush remaining mustard mixture evenly over tops and sides of cabbage wedges. Cover sheet tightly with aluminum foil and roast for 10 minutes.

**3** Remove foil and brush tops and sides of cabbage wedges with reserved mustard mixture. Return to oven and roast uncovered until cabbage is tender when pierced with paring knife and browned around edges, 15 to 18 minutes. Sprinkle with parsley and serve.

# Chapter 6

# Drinks and Snacks

Pineapple-Peach Tea

Ginger-Orange Soda

Brazilian Lemonade

Secret Red Sangria

Goat Cheese–Stuffed Olives

Prosciutto–Goat Cheese Logs with
Honey and Rosemary

Candied Prosciutto

Air-Fried Barbecue Chickpeas

Air-Fried Roasted Salsa

Crab Salad Pastry Puffs

Onion Jam and Goat Cheese
Flatbread

Candied Walnuts

Sparkling Whipped Cream Dip
with Berries

Sweet Potato Pie Dip

Brown Sugar Caramel Sauce

# Pineapple-Peach Tea

**Makes:** 8 drinks   ·   **Total time:** 50 minutes

*Whenever I'm entertaining, I love to offer a signature drink to pair with the meal. It's a great way to add something special to the menu, and my guests always enjoy it. Frozen fruit is one of my must-have pantry staples because it's such an easy and convenient path to any number of flavor-packed drinks. Here, by cooking down the thawed pineapple and peaches with some sugar, you get a delicious fruity syrup that infuses flavor into black tea as it steeps. (And you could swap in green tea bags instead, if you like.) Then, just strain out the solids and serve. Oh, and one of my favorite things about this drink? It's equally delicious served hot or cold.*

10   ounces frozen pineapple chunks, thawed

10   ounces frozen sliced peaches, thawed

1   cup granulated sugar, divided

8   cups water

2   black tea bags

**1**   Combine pineapple, peaches, and ⅓ cup sugar in large saucepan. Cook over medium heat until fruit is softened and juices have thickened slightly, about 30 minutes.

**2**   Stir in water and remaining ⅔ cup sugar and bring to simmer. Add tea bags, reduce heat to medium-low, and cook until sugar is dissolved and flavors meld, 7 to 10 minutes.

**3**   Remove saucepan from heat. Gently squeeze tea bags to extract as much liquid as possible, then discard. Strain mixture through fine-mesh strainer into large container, pressing on solids to extract as much liquid as possible; discard solids. Serve hot, or let cool to room temperature and serve over ice.

## *Pantry Pick*

**Frozen fruit:** The fruit section of the freezer aisle doesn't get enough love. Going frozen lets you enjoy high-quality seasonal fruit, from wild blueberries to mangos to peaches, year-round, since the fruit is frozen at peak ripeness. And going frozen instead of using whole fresh fruit can save you prep time.

### *Antoinette's Tip*

Get creative and swap out the pineapple and peaches for other frozen fruit: Try a strawberry-blackberry combo or a mango-raspberry pairing.

## Antoinette's Tips

I love using blood oranges in this soda when I can get them, but you can use any kind of orange that you like and that looks good at the supermarket.

Use leftover brown sugar simple syrup to sweeten iced coffee, iced tea, cocktails, or even breakfast oatmeal.

# Ginger-Orange Soda

**Makes:** 2 drinks  ·  **Total time:** 10 minutes

*When I make my weekly (or sometimes daily) grocery store runs, I head to the discounted produce section first. There isn't always something worth buying, but when there is, it can be a gem. One time I lucked out and got a full bag of beautiful blood oranges for only 99 cents. They were sweet and juicy and had so much depth of flavor—yet I knew that I would need to finish the bag fast, before the oranges went bad. This is how the first iteration of my Ginger-Orange Soda was birthed. I've since refined and updated the recipe, adding fresh grated ginger instead of ground to provide its distinctive spiciness to this effervescent and sweet drink. The ginger is complemented by the rich-tasting simple syrup made with dark brown sugar (and you'll have leftover syrup for making future batches of soda). As simple as this is to prepare, I feel swanky and sophisticated whenever I make this bubbly beverage. This recipe makes two drinks, but you can easily double, triple, or even quadruple it! Your guests will thank you.*

1   cup packed dark brown sugar

1   cup warm tap water

¼   cup plus 2 tablespoons orange juice

½   teaspoon grated fresh ginger

1½   cups lemon seltzer, divided

**1**   Whisk sugar and warm water in bowl until sugar has dissolved. Let cool completely. (Simple syrup can be refrigerated for up to 1 month.)

**2**   Add ¼ cup brown sugar simple syrup, orange juice, and ginger to cocktail shaker, then fill with ice. Shake mixture until just combined and chilled, about 5 seconds. Strain drink into 2 chilled pint glasses half-filled with ice. Add 6 ounces seltzer to each glass and, using spoon, gently lift orange mixture from bottom of glass to top to combine. Top with additional ice. Serve.

# Brazilian Lemonade

**Makes:** 5 drinks  ·  **Total time:** 15 minutes

*The discipline it takes to NOT scroll Instagram during the wee hours of the night is something I don't have. And I'm okay with that. Why? Because nine times out of ten when I'm having these late-night scroll sessions, I come across a recipe that gets my mind going. Known in Portuguese as limonada Suíça, Brazilian lemonade uses WHOLE limes (limonada translates into English as "lemonade"). Blending condensed milk and WHOLE limes together to create a frothy and refreshing drink was something I could not fathom. So many thoughts went racing through my mind: How will this work? Won't it taste bitter? Condensed milk in a drink? I also had a flashback to a Cook's Country cake recipe that was made with WHOLE clementines blended into a cake batter and sliced and candied WHOLE clementines on top. I keep capitalizing the word WHOLE because the idea seems so strange to me, but it works! Because I love that cake recipe, I decided to add thin-skinned mandarins to my take on Brazilian lemonade. The result is a beverage that's tart-sweet, creamy, and very refreshing.*

4    cups water

3    limes, quartered

3    mandarin oranges, quartered

⅓    cup sweetened condensed milk

⅓    cup granulated sugar

**1**    Combine water, limes, mandarins, condensed milk, and sugar in blender jar. Pulse mixture 5 times, then process on low for 10 seconds. Increase speed to high and process until fruit pieces are no larger than grains of rice, 1 to 2 minutes.

**2**    Strain fruit mixture through fine-mesh strainer and discard pulp. Transfer strained juice to pitcher. Serve over ice.

## Antoinette's Tips

Since you use the whole citrus fruit, be sure to scrub them with warm water first.

You can use clementines or tangerines if you can't find mandarins.

For extra razzle-dazzle, add coconut rum or tequila to taste.

## *Antoinette's Tips*

For the OJ in this recipe, you can use reconstituted frozen juice, juice from a carton, or even freshly squeezed. They all work!

Choose a fresh and fruity young red wine for your sangria—this is not the time to go for an earthy or oaky bottle. I often use merlot. Another great choice would be garnacha.

# Secret Red Sangria

**Makes:** 14 cocktails · **Total time:** 15 minutes

*Get ready to raise your glasses and say hello to the magical powers of canned concentrated juice! I know what you're thinking—canned juice in sangria? But trust me, it's a game-changer. Because the grape juice concentrate is intense in fruity flavor and sweetness, it holds up better in this boozier recipe. While some sangria recipes might contain brandy and/or triple sec, I like to make my secret recipe (well, I guess it's not so secret anymore) with bourbon. Plus I also add triple sec for good measure. Whether you're lounging by the pool on a hot day, hosting a spontaneous gathering, or just craving an indulgent refresher, my quick and delicious sangria recipe has got your back. Grab your pitcher, pop open that can of concentrated juice, and let the good times flow. Cheers to simplicity!*

1½ cups packed dark brown sugar

1½ cups warm tap water

2 (750-ml) bottles red wine

1 (12-ounce) can frozen grape juice concentrate

1 cup bourbon

1 cup orange juice

½ cup triple sec

1 orange, sliced into ¼-inch-thick rounds

**1** Whisk sugar and warm water in bowl until sugar has dissolved. Let cool completely.

**2** Combine cooled brown sugar simple syrup, wine, grape juice concentrate, bourbon, orange juice, triple sec, and orange slices in serving pitcher and stir well. Serve in glasses half-filled with ice.

## *Pantry Pick*

**Frozen juice concentrate:** Frozen concentrated juice (look for 100% juice) takes up little space, keeps for literally years in your freezer, and is less expensive than bottled juice. Why *wouldn't* you keep this product on hand?

# Goat Cheese–Stuffed Olives

**Serves:** 8 to 10 (makes about 26 stuffed olives)
**Total time:** 20 minutes

*Let's set the scene. You've been invited to a party and asked to contribute a snack. Arriving with something premade from the store isn't an acceptable option, but you really don't have the time or patience to cook something. What do you do? Make these cheesy stuffed olives and you're sure to receive accolades from your fellow party guests. This two-ingredient recipe is simple, tastes delicious, and gives the illusion of being a labor-intensive dish, when in reality it's so easy. First, you want to use giant or colossal olives, because regular-size ones are too small and you will go crazy trying to stuff them. Second, for a one-stop filling, use seasoned goat cheese. I like herbed goat cheese here, but feel free to get creative and experiment with other savory goat cheese flavors, including cheese flavored with chiles, spices, sun-dried tomatoes, or even truffles.*

| | |
|---|---|
| 2 | ounces garlic and herb goat cheese, softened (½ cup) |
| 1½ | cups large pitted Castelvetrano olives |

Transfer goat cheese to small zipper-lock bag and snip off corner to make hole about ¼ inch wide. Squeeze cheese mixture out of hole in bag into hole into each olive, filling each olive completely. Serve.

## *Pantry Pick*

**Jarred olives:** Look for 1-inch-long pitted olives, as this large size will make stuffing them a lot less fiddly. The test kitchen likes Mezzetta Colossal Castelvetrano Style Pitted Olives, which have a mild flavor that works well with the goat cheese.

## Antoinette's Tip

Make sure your cheeses are softened for easy mixing. Even more important, using softened cheese will prevent the precious prosciutto from tearing when you try to spread the filling mixture on the slices.

# Prosciutto-Goat Cheese Logs with Honey and Rosemary

**Serves:** 6 to 8 as an appetizer   ·   **Total time:** 10 minutes

*This party snack is full of flavor, mingling saltiness from the prosciutto, sweetness from the honey, and tanginess from the goat cheese. It's an elevated no-cook appetizer that's great for a gathering—but I think these little logs are even better when you get to enjoy them all by yourself. Best of all, it all comes together quickly with just a few items from the deli section. I use fresh rosemary here, rather than dried, because it has a light piney flavor that just works really well with the cheeses, ham, and honey. You'll want to use a very sharp knife for cutting the prosciutto, as this will produce clean cuts and prevent the prosciutto from snagging. I like to pop the assembled logs into the fridge for 30 minutes to chill after preparing them, but you should feel free to dig in right away, if you prefer.*

2  ounces goat cheese, softened

2  ounces cream cheese, softened

1  teaspoon honey

½  teaspoon minced fresh rosemary

4  ounces thinly sliced prosciutto, halved crosswise

Place goat cheese, cream cheese, honey, and rosemary in bowl and mash with fork until well combined. Spread 1 teaspoon goat cheese mixture evenly over bottom 1 inch of short side of 1 prosciutto slice, then roll into tight log around goat cheese. Repeat with remaining prosciutto slices and remaining goat cheese. Serve.

# Candied Prosciutto

**Serves:** 6 to 8 as an appetizer  ·  **Total time:** 30 minutes

*The origins of this recipe come from my time competing on America's Test Kitchen: The Next Generation. During episode 4, I was tasked with making a black tie–themed charcuterie board in 60 minutes, and one of the items I prepared was Champagne candied prosciutto. Not only was it a big hit, but it was also quick to make and took minimal effort. For this version, I streamlined the recipe by leaving out the Champagne (though I encourage you to serve it alongside, in flute glasses!). If you're like me and consider prosciutto a must-have pantry ingredient, you may already have everything you need at home. (And if you don't consider prosciutto a must-have pantry ingredient, you should!) This crispy and crackly, salty and sweet snack is an amazing addition to a savory board. I'll confess, though, that I've been known to eat these tidbits on their own, like chips.*

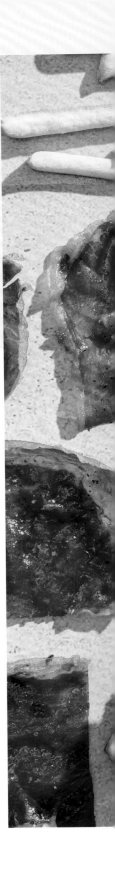

| | |
|---|---|
| 4 | teaspoons packed dark brown sugar |
| ½ | teaspoon pepper |
| ⅛ | teaspoon table salt |
| 4 | ounces thinly sliced prosciutto, halved crosswise |
| 1 | teaspoon extra-virgin olive oil |

**1**  Adjust oven racks to upper-middle and lower-middle positions and heat oven to 375 degrees. Combine sugar, pepper, and salt in small bowl. Line 2 rimmed baking sheets with parchment paper and spray with vegetable oil spray. Arrange prosciutto slices in single layer over prepared sheets, then brush top side of prosciutto with oil and sprinkle with sugar mixture. (Do not flip prosciutto and coat second side.)

**2**  Bake until sugar is bubbling and prosciutto is dark brown, 8 to 10 minutes, switching and rotating sheets halfway through baking. Let cool on sheet for 5 minutes. Serve.

### Antoinette's Tip

Given the sugar on the prosciutto, you should monitor the slices closely as they bake—they can go from burnished to black in no time.

# Air-Fried Barbecue Chickpeas

**Serves:** 4 (makes 1 cup)  ·  **Total time:** 50 minutes

*Ignite your taste buds with a smoky, crispy snack that will keep you reaching for more. First, let's talk about its simplicity. With just a handful of ingredients and a couple of easy steps, you'll have a crunchy snack that beats any store-bought treat. We're taking humble canned chickpeas and giving them a mouthwatering makeover by coating them with my Barbecue Spice Rub and some extra-virgin olive oil. As they cook in the air fryer, they absorb the barbecue flavors and transform into irresistible bites of deliciousness. Now, let's talk about this recipe's versatility. Break these out when you're hosting a casual gathering with drinks, craving a satisfying afternoon snack, or when you need to jazz up a lunchtime salad.*

1  (15-ounce) can chickpeas, rinsed and patted dry

2  tablespoons Barbecue Spice Rub (page 55)

1  tablespoon extra-virgin olive oil

Toss chickpeas, barbecue spice rub, and oil in large bowl until chickpeas are evenly coated. Transfer chickpeas to air fryer basket. Place basket into air fryer and set temperature to 300 degrees. Cook until chickpeas are shrunken and crispy, 30 to 40 minutes, stirring every 10 minutes. Let cool completely, about 15 minutes, before serving (chickpeas will continue to crisp as they cool).

## Antoinette's Tip

You can substitute your favorite store-bought barbecue
spice mix for the homemade version, if you prefer.

# Air-Fried Roasted Salsa

**Serves:** 6 to 8 (makes 1¾ cups) · **Total time:** 25 minutes, plus 4 hours chilling

*You may ask, why make your own salsa when there are so many brands and flavors on grocery store shelves? Because making your own salsa lets you control the ingredients, customize the heat level, and save money too. Roasting your vegetables—easy to do in the air fryer—intensifies their flavors and adds a smoky note to your finished salsa, making it more complex than any processed store-bought version. At the end of the roasting session, your veggies should be nicely charred and fragrant from the garlic. This flavor-packed salsa is reminiscent in texture of a thinner, restaurant-style salsa.*

6    plum tomatoes, cored

1    jalapeño, stemmed and seeded

1    shallot, halved

2    garlic cloves, peeled

1½   tablespoons lime juice

1½   teaspoons table salt

2    tablespoons minced fresh cilantro

**1**   Place tomatoes, jalapeño, shallot, and garlic in air fryer basket. Place basket in air fryer and set temperature to 400 degrees. Cook until beginning to char, 12 to 15 minutes.

**2**   Transfer jalapeño, shallot, and garlic to cutting board and chop coarse. Transfer to blender and pulse until vegetable pieces are no larger than ½ inch, about 10 pulses. Add tomatoes, lime juice, and salt and pulse until tomatoes are broken down and mostly smooth and vegetable pieces are no larger than ¼ inch, about 10 pulses. Transfer salsa to bowl and stir in cilantro. Cover and refrigerate for at least 4 hours or up to 24 hours. Serve.

## *Pantry Pick*

**Limes:** Most of us probably keep a lemon in the fridge for spritzing over various foods when the mood strikes. But don't overlook limes—they do a lot more than garnish a drink! Their tart, subtly bitter flavor livens up this salsa. And here's a fun fact: Limes are actually higher in vitamin C than lemons.

# Crab Salad Pastry Puffs

**Serves:** 4 to 6 (makes 9 pastry squares)  ·  **Total time:** 30 minutes

*There is something about recipes with crab that immediately makes me think, "Oh this is fancy." When turned into a creamy salad and tucked into light and flaky puff pastry shells, it seems to me like elegance on a plate, and my taste buds can barely handle the explosion of flavor. This is a fabulous recipe to break out when you want to impress your guests without exerting too much effort. These puffs will make you feel like you're attending a proper Southern tea—even if you're only sitting on your couch binge-watching your favorite TV show.*

1   (9½ by 9-inch) sheet puff pastry, thawed

¼   cup minced celery

3   tablespoon mayonnaise

2   tablespoons finely chopped red bell pepper

1   teaspoon Dijon mustard

1   teaspoon lemon juice

1   teaspoon garlic powder

½   teaspoon table salt

½   teaspoon Old Bay seasoning

8   ounces lump crabmeat, picked over for shells and large pieces flaked

**1**   Adjust oven rack to middle position and heat oven to 400 degrees. Line rimmed baking sheet with parchment paper. Unfold puff pastry and cut into nine 3-inch squares. Arrange squares about ½ inch apart on prepared sheet and bake until golden brown, 10 to 14 minutes. Transfer sheet to wire rack and let puff pastry squares cool completely.

**2**   Combine celery, mayonnaise, bell pepper, mustard, lemon juice, garlic powder, salt, and Old Bay in medium bowl. Gently fold in crabmeat. Using tip of paring knife, cut ½-inch-wide border around top edge of each pastry, then press centers down with your fingertips to create indentation. Divide crab mixture evenly over center of cooled pastry shells. Serve immediately.

## *Pantry Picks*

**Puff pastry:** Let's be real; no one is making their own puff pastry unless they're a pastry chef. Why wouldn't you have this modern miracle of a convenience product in your freezer at all times? My other favorite way to use puff pastry is in Pigs on a Blanket (page 200).

**Canned crab:** You might see "lump," "backfin," or "claw" specified on canned crabmeat. Try to buy lump crabmeat, which has smaller pieces of jumbo lump crab and a delicate flavor. The test kitchen's favorite canned crabmeat is Miller's Select Lump Crab Meat. You can also use refrigerated packaged crab; the test kitchen likes Phillips Premium Crab Jumbo.

### Antoinette's Tip

To thaw frozen puff pastry, let it sit either in the refrigerator for 24 hours or on the counter for 30 minutes to 1 hour.

# Onion Jam and Goat Cheese Flatbread

**Serves:** 8 to 10 as an appetizer · **Total time:** 40 minutes

*This quick and impressive crowd-pleaser will instantly elevate your entertaining game and will have your guests begging for more. (Luckily, it's easy enough to double this recipe to make two flatbreads.) Thanks to the supreme convenience of store-bought pizza dough and premade jarred onion jam (one of my favorite condiments), you can whip up this hearty handheld appetizer in no time. The best part? Just five ingredients come together to make something as sophisticated as it is effortless. For another recipe that uses onion jam, check out Not Your Mother's Meatloaf (page 147).*

1 pound pizza dough, room temperature

½ cup caramelized onion jam

6 ounces andouille sausage, sliced ¼ inch thick

4 ounces goat cheese, crumbled (1 cup)

1½ teaspoons fresh thyme leaves

## *Pantry Pick*

### Andouille sausage:

This traditional Louisiana smoked sausage is made from pork, garlic, and lots of black pepper and is used in gumbo and jambalaya. It brings huge flavor to any dish. Wellshire is a nationally available brand that the test kitchen recommends.

**1** Adjust oven rack to lowest position and heat oven to 500 degrees. Spray rimmed baking sheet with vegetable oil spray. Press and roll dough into 15 by 11-inch rectangle on lightly floured counter. (If dough springs back, roll into as large a rectangle as possible, then let rest on counter for 5 more minutes before continuing to roll out.) Transfer dough to prepared sheet and press to edges of sheet. Bake dough until puffy and golden brown in spots, about 5 minutes.

**2** Remove crust from oven and press flat any large bubbles with spatula. Spread onion jam over surface of dough, leaving ½-inch border around edge. Arrange sausage over crust, then sprinkle with goat cheese.

**3** Bake flatbread until cheese is softened and crust is golden around edges, 10 to 15 minutes. Let cool for 5 minutes, then sprinkle with thyme, cut into slices, and serve.

# Candied Walnuts

**Serves:** 8 (makes 2 cups)  ·  **Total time:** 55 minutes

*Fill your kitchen with the sweet aroma of nostalgia with my oven-baked spiced sweet walnuts. This recipe pays homage to the love of my mother, with some inspiration taken from my holiday mall walks as well. My version of candied nuts cuts out the messy stovetop caramelization process—you just stir everything together, spread it on a baking sheet, and pop it in the oven. To achieve the perfect crunch and irresistible sweetness, I take a cue from the test kitchen and harness the power of an egg white. As the walnuts bake in the oven, the egg white, mixed with the sugar and spices, creates a delicate and crispy coating. These also make an amazing topping for my No-Churn Sweet Potato Pie Ice Cream (page 43).*

| | |
|---|---|
| 1 | large egg white |
| ¾ | cup (5¼ ounces) sugar |
| ½ | teaspoon ground ginger |
| ½ | teaspoon ground allspice |
| ½ | teaspoon ground cinnamon |
| ¼ | teaspoon table salt |
| 2 | cups walnuts |

**1**  Adjust oven rack to middle position and heat oven to 350 degrees. Line rimmed baking sheet with parchment paper. Whisk egg white in bowl until frothy, about 30 seconds. Add sugar, ginger, allspice, cinnamon, and salt and whisk until combined. Add walnuts and stir to evenly coat.

**2**  Transfer walnuts to prepared sheet and spread into single layer. Bake until walnuts are fragrant and deeply browned, 20 to 25 minutes, stirring halfway through. Transfer nuts to large plate and let cool completely, about 20 minutes. Serve. (Walnuts can be stored at room temperature in airtight container for up to 1 week.)

## *Pantry Pick*

**Walnuts:** I love the rich, earthy flavor of walnuts. Their very slight natural bitterness is perfectly offset by candying them with sugar and spices. Along with peanuts, these are the nuts I most often have stashed in my freezer.

### Antoinette's Tip

This snack is just as delicious made with pecans, pistachios, almonds, or cashews instead of the walnuts—or try a mix of multiple nuts.

# Sparkling Whipped Cream Dip with Berries

**Serves:** 8 to 10 (makes 2½ cups)  ·  **Total time:** 10 minutes

*I haven't been to a party, gathering, or get-together that didn't have some sort of dip on the menu. Dips are quintessential party foods and a great go-to when entertaining. However, you often see repeats of the same small savory selection. A fun way to combat this is to go sweet! I love bringing a dessert dip to the party because of the positive reaction it always receives. This prosecco-flavored whipped cream with fresh berries sounds fancy, but it's so fast and easy that it will become your new go-to. You could use an equal amount of vanilla extract here, but the vanilla bean paste provides a taste you can see, lightly speckling the whipped cream, and I love that. Make sure your bowl, heavy cream, and prosecco are cold. This will aid in keeping the whipped cream stable.*

2    ounces cream cheese, softened

¼    cup (1 ounce) confectioners' sugar

1    teaspoon vanilla bean paste

1    cup heavy cream

⅓    cup sparkling wine, such as prosecco

Strawberries

Using stand mixer fitted with whisk attachment, whip cream cheese, sugar, and vanilla bean paste on medium speed until well combined, about 1 minute. Add cream and sparkling wine and whip on medium-low speed until foamy, about 1 minute. Increase speed to high and whip until stiff peaks form, 1 to 3 minutes. Serve with strawberries. (Whipped cream can be refrigerated in airtight container for 2 hours.)

## *Pantry Pick*

**Cream cheese:** It's a hero in this recipe. It may sound a little odd if you've never done it, but whenever I make whipped cream, I always add some softened cream cheese. It adds tangy flavor and also helps prevent the whipped cream from collapsing.

## Antoinette's Tips

I love to serve the whipped cream like a dip, accompanied by whole strawberries or peach wedges. It's also fun to dollop the whipped cream into individual dessert glasses and top it with sliced strawberries or smaller whole berries like blackberries or raspberries.

A stand mixer will whip the cream faster, but you can use a hand mixer if you prefer.

## Antoinette's Tip

Using a hand mixer is more efficient than breaking out
your stand mixer for this recipe.

# Sweet Potato Pie Dip

**Serves:** 8 to 10 (makes 2⅓ cups)  ·  **Total time:** 15 minutes, plus 2 hours chilling

*This quick dessert has all the flavors of sweet potato pie—without any of the baking! Like the Sparkling Whipped Cream Dip with Berries (page 186), this is a sweet dip that I love to make for any get-together; plus, you can make it several hours ahead. It's great for the holidays, of course, but delicious any time of year. The cream cheese is here for both its tangy flavor and its practical function, helping to create a firmer texture that mimics sweet potato pie filling. I do love the vanilla bean paste in this, but you could sub in an equal amount of vanilla extract instead. My favorite accompaniments for this dip are Biscoff cookies and gingersnaps. You can also serve this with graham crackers, vanilla wafers, shortbread, or pizzelle.*

2   ounces cream cheese, cut into 4 pieces and softened

¼   cup sweetened condensed milk

2   tablespoons packed dark brown sugar

2   teaspoons granulated sugar

1   teaspoon vanilla bean paste

¼   teaspoon ground cinnamon

¼   teaspoon ground nutmeg

¼   teaspoon ground allspice

⅛   teaspoon ground ginger

Pinch table salt

1   (15-ounce) can sweet potato puree

**1**   Using hand mixer set at medium speed, beat cream cheese, condensed milk, brown sugar, granulated sugar, vanilla bean paste, cinnamon, nutmeg, allspice, ginger, and salt in large bowl until well combined and fluffy, about 2 minutes.

**2**   Add sweet potato puree and beat until well combined, about 1 minute. Transfer to serving dish, cover with plastic wrap, and refrigerate for 2 hours (or up to 8 hours) before serving.

## *Pantry Pick*

**Baking spices:** Cinnamon, nutmeg, allspice, and ginger are the core baking spices that I always have on hand, for pies, cakes, baked fruit desserts—and this dip! You can actually buy jars of these spices premixed under the name "baking spice" (or "pumpkin pie spice," which subs cloves for allspice), but I prefer to keep separate jars on hand so I can customize their balance of sweet, woodsy, earthy flavors.

# Brown Sugar Caramel Sauce

**Serves:** 8 (makes 1 cup)  ·  **Total time:** 15 minutes

Drizzle, dip, and dive into this failproof caramel sauce. This recipe requires no candy thermometer or complex techniques, making it a breeze even for novice cooks. It outshines anything you can buy in the store, and it's so fast that you can make it anytime the urge strikes. Dark brown sugar, butter, and cream transform into a velvety concoction that oozes with indulgence, and a pinch of salt heightens the flavors. Say goodbye to the fear of burnt sugar and hello to a caramel sauce that's as easy as it is heavenly!

½   cup packed (3½ ounces) dark brown sugar

2   tablespoons unsalted butter

½   cup heavy cream

Pinch table salt

**1**   Combine sugar and butter in small saucepan. Cook over medium heat until butter is melted and sugar is evenly moistened, 2 to 3 minutes, stirring frequently.

**2**   While whisking constantly, slowly add cream. Increase heat to medium-high and bring to boil, whisking frequently. Once boiling, remove from heat and stir in salt.

**3**   Transfer to serving dish or bowl and let cool slightly, about 5 minutes. Serve. (Caramel can be refrigerated in airtight container for up to 1 week.)

## Antoinette's Tip

This versatile sauce isn't just for ice cream. Drizzle it over cheesecake, apple pie, or brownies. Swirl it into hot chocolate or coffee. You can even use it as a dip for fresh fruits. Possibilities are endless, and satisfaction is guaranteed.

# Chapter 7

# Mostly Homemade Classics, Updated

Overnight Breakfast Casserole

Strawberry-Hoisin Meatballs

Sausage Balls with Lime-Cilantro Dipping Sauce

Pigs on a Blanket

Barbecue Chicken Leg Quarters

Carolina-Style Cheeseburgers

Queso Dip

Cheesy Garlic Hawaiian Rolls

Lemon-Blueberry Dump Crumble

# Overnight Breakfast Casserole

**Serves:** 8 to 12  ·  **Total time:** 1¼ hours, plus up to 18 hours chilling and 20 minutes resting (if prepping the day before)

*Overnight breakfast egg casseroles, often made with bread cubes or shredded potatoes and sausage, have been around for a loooong time. They bring back warm memories of my child-hood, when my mom would prepare her version whenever we had family staying over. My hassle-free updated recipe is assembled in less than 15 minutes, so you can easily prep it the night before and then just pop it into the oven in the a.m. to bake while you do other things. Or if you prefer, you can do the assembly and baking all at once, in the morning. With layers of crispy hash brown patties, sharp cheddar cheese, smoky diced ham, and zesty green chiles, all soaked in a hot sauce–spiked egg mixture, this casserole is a hearty way to start the day. So gather your loved ones and make memories as you savor this comforting favorite.*

| | |
|---|---|
| 8 | frozen hash brown patties |
| 8 | ounces sharp cheddar cheese, shredded (2 cups) |
| 1 | (8-ounce) package diced ham |
| ½ | cup canned chopped green chiles |
| 2 | cups milk |
| 6 | large eggs |
| 1 | tablespoon hot sauce |
| 1 | teaspoon table salt |
| ½ | teaspoon garlic powder |
| ½ | teaspoon onion powder |
| ¼ | teaspoon pepper |

**1**  Grease 13 by 9-inch baking dish. Arrange hash brown patties in single layer over bottom of prepared dish, then sprinkle evenly with cheese, ham, and green chiles. Whisk milk, eggs, hot sauce, salt, garlic powder, onion powder, and pepper together in large bowl, then pour over hash browns. Cover dish with aluminum foil and refrigerate for up to 18 hours.

**2**  Adjust oven rack to middle position and heat oven to 350 degrees. Remove dish from refrigerator, discard foil, and let sit at room temperature for 20 minutes (while oven heats). Bake casserole until edges are browned and top is set, about 50 minutes. Transfer to wire rack and let cool for 10 minutes. Serve.

## *Pantry Pick*

**Hash brown patties:** While prepackaged frozen hash browns (peeled and shredded or cubed potatoes) are a wonderful convenience product, frozen hash brown patties take the ease one step further by being already cooked and formed into patties. All you need to do is heat and eat.

## Antoinette's Tips

This recipe was designed to be a gift to yourself the next morning, but if you're in a breakfast-for-dinner kind of mood, you can bake this immediately after assembling it.

If you can't find diced ham, you can substitute 8 ounces ham steak, cut into ¼-inch pieces.

# Strawberry-Hoisin Meatballs

**Serves:** 10 to 12 as an appetizer  ·  **Total time:** 20 minutes

*Southerners expect mini meatballs when they attend a baby shower—it's a long-held custom. Traditionally, these meatballs are made in the slow cooker using frozen meatballs, grape jelly, and barbecue sauce (or a tomato-based chili sauce), which sounds odd but which creates a tangy, sweet-and-smoky sauce. Here's my twist on those classic baby shower meatballs that everyone knows and loves, and I'm bringing some Chinese flair to the party. I know it also might sound odd to pair straw-berry preserves with hoisin sauce, but is it any more so than grape jelly and barbecue sauce? Trust me, it's not—and taking this recipe out of the slow cooker means you'll have these meatballs ready to devour in no time, without sacrificing any of the simplicity of the original. Although I often break this out for entertaining, you could also serve the meatballs over rice to make a meal. Either way, you'll be the talk of the town!*

¾ cup hoisin sauce

½ cup strawberry preserves

¼ cup water

20 ounces frozen meatballs (½ ounce each)

Whisk hoisin, strawberry preserves, and water together in medium saucepan. Stir in frozen meatballs and bring to simmer over medium heat. Cover, and cook, stirring frequently, until meatballs are warmed through, about 10 minutes. Serve.

## Antoinette's Tip

For a true Southern experience, make sure you buy
½-ounce mini meatballs for this recipe. I buy "homestyle"
meatballs for this dish rather than Italian-style or other
flavored meatballs.

## Antoinette's Tips

I use Bisquick Original Pancake and Baking Mix, but there are plenty of other good brands out there.

Although you can combine the dough ingredients by hand, a stand mixer will effortlessly create a homogenous mixture with the sticky sausage. A 4.5-quart head-tilt mixer will be quite full, so start out slow when mixing.

# Sausage Balls with Lime-Cilantro Dipping Sauce

**Serves:** 12 to 14 (makes 38 sausage balls)   ·   **Total time:** 45 minutes

*I guess Southerners like poppable little meaty bites, because, like the Strawberry-Hoisin Meatballs on page 196, these savory sausage balls are often served for celebrations, especially around holiday time. They're also a cocktail-party and game-day favorite. Sausage balls are often made with breakfast-style or sweet Italian sausage and cheddar cheese, but here I take a flavor detour to the Southwest by using chorizo sausage and Monterey Jack cheese, pairing the baked sausage balls with a tangy sour cream dipping sauce flavored with lime and cilantro. They're a breeze to make, thanks to the magic of pancake and baking mix—a store-bought shortcut that I can't resist.*

2   cups sour cream

¼   cup minced fresh cilantro

1   tablespoon lime zest plus
    4 teaspoons juice

½   teaspoon table salt

1   pound Mexican-style chorizo
    sausage, casings removed

2   cups pancake and baking mix

1   pound Monterey Jack cheese,
    shredded (4 cups)

**1**   Adjust oven rack to middle position and heat oven to 350 degrees. Combine sour cream, cilantro, lime zest and juice, and salt in bowl. Refrigerate sauce until ready to serve.

**2**   Line rimmed baking sheet with aluminum foil and set wire rack in sheet; spray rack with vegetable oil spray. Using stand mixer fitted with paddle attachment, mix sausage and pancake mix on low speed until combined, about 1 minute. Add cheese and continue to mix on low speed until incorporated, 30 seconds to 1 minute.

**3**   Roll into thirty-eight 1½-inch-wide balls (about 2 tablespoons each) and space ½ inch apart on prepared rack. Bake until meatballs are golden brown and register 160 degrees, about 20 minutes. Transfer to serving dish and let cool for 5 minutes. Serve with dipping sauce.

## *Pantry Pick*

**Mexican chorizo:** This fresh pork sausage, available in links or bulk form, is bright red from spicy red pepper. You can cook or grill the links whole or remove the meat from the casings and use it in these sausage balls, burgers, or tacos.

# Pigs on a Blanket

**Serves:** 3 or 4 (makes 9 squares)  ·  **Total time:** 50 minutes

*I take this retro finger food and childhood favorite to a whole new level by swapping out the ordinary crescent rolls (and the fiddly wrapping step) for flaky, buttery, decidedly grown-up puff pastry squares and using garlicky andouille sausage instead of cocktail franks. Trust me, these simple switch-ups will take your taste buds on a familiar yet all-new journey. As long as you've thawed the puff pastry properly, it's easy to assemble these little bites of heaven. First, cut the pastry into squares. Then layer on some store-bought caramelized onion jam—a sweet and savory pantry-friendly delight that adds a big burst of flavor (see page 147 for more info). Finally, arrange rounds of andouille sausage on top and pop them into the oven. In no time, you'll have golden-brown, surprisingly sophisticated pigs on blankets that are ready to be devoured.*

1 (9½ by 9-inch) sheet puff pastry, thawed

6 tablespoons caramelized onion jam

3½ ounces andouille sausage, cut into ¼-inch-thick rounds

**1** Adjust oven rack to middle position and heat oven to 400 degrees. Line rimmed baking sheet with parchment paper. Unfold puff pastry and cut into nine 3-inch squares. Arrange squares about ½ inch apart on prepared sheet.

**2** Divide onion jam evenly among centers of each pastry (about 2 teaspoons each), spreading into even layer and leaving ½-inch border on all sides. Arrange sausage pieces in a row, overlapping as needed to remain within border and on top of onion jam.

**3** Bake until edges are golden brown, about 20 minutes. Let cool on sheet for 10 minutes. Serve warm.

### Antoinette's Tip

To thaw frozen puff pastry, let it sit either in the refrigerator for 24 hours or on the counter for 30 minutes to 1 hour.

# Barbecue Chicken Leg Quarters

**Serves:** 4 · **Total time:** 55 minutes

*Barbecue chicken is an old standby, right? Well, not when you use my homemade spice rub and roast chicken leg quarters rather than chicken breasts. Chicken leg quarters are budget-friendly and versatile—and they deliver a succulent dining experience that doesn't compromise on flavor. Roasting them at a high temperature helps to create a crispy exterior while sealing in the juices for tender meat. Thanks to their darker meat and higher fat content, there's no danger of them drying out like chicken breasts are prone to do. To take advantage of the simplicity and versatility of this recipe, repurpose leftovers (or double the recipe) for other delectable meals. Shred any remaining meat and use it to create tacos, salads, sandwiches, and more. It's a fantastic and simple way to stretch your ingredients and create new and exciting meals.*

¼ cup Barbecue Spice Rub (page 55)

2 teaspoons table salt

4 (10- to 12-ounce) chicken leg quarters, trimmed

**1** Adjust oven rack to middle position and heat oven to 425 degrees. Combine barbecue spice rub and salt in small bowl. Pat chicken dry with paper towels, then rub all over with spice rub mixture, gently lifting skin to distribute spice rub underneath but leaving it attached to chicken.

**2** Transfer chicken, skin side up, to wire rack set in aluminum foil-lined rimmed baking sheet. Roast until chicken is well browned and registers at least 175 degrees, 35 to 40 minutes.

**3** Transfer chicken to platter and let rest for 5 minutes. Serve.

### Antoinette's Tip

Because there are only three ingredients here, I definitely recommend using my homemade spice rub. You can substitute your favorite store-bought rub, if you prefer.

# Carolina-Style Cheeseburgers

**Serves:** 4 · **Total time:** 35 minutes

*Growing up in North Carolina, I developed a deep appreciation for the unique culinary traditions of the region. Carolina-style cheeseburgers (and Carolina chili dogs) are a beloved and iconic local favorite, featuring a bold combination of tangy, smoky, and savory flavors. "Carolina-style" refers to the toppings: The beef patty (or hot dog) is topped with beef chili sauce, coleslaw, and onions (and sometimes mustard). It's a messy delight to eat, but all the components can take some time to prepare. So I created a fast, simplified burger that contains all the seasonings of the chili and onion right in the burger patty. Topped with sliced cheese and vinegary slaw, this burger embodies all the flavors I love, and I'm excited and proud to share the recipe with you.*

1   pound 80 percent lean ground beef

⅓   cup grated onion

2   tablespoons yellow mustard

2   tablespoons ketchup

1   tablespoon chili powder

1   teaspoon table salt, divided

1   teaspoon vegetable oil

4   thin slices deli cheddar cheese (4 ounces)

½   cup mayonnaise

¼   cup cider vinegar

1   tablespoon sugar

¼   teaspoon pepper

6   ounces (2 cups) green coleslaw mix

4   hamburger buns

**1**   Combine ground beef, onion, mustard, ketchup, chili powder, and ¾ teaspoon salt in bowl. Knead gently with your hands until well combined. Divide into 4 equal portions, then gently shape each portion into ¾-inch-thick patties. Using your fingertips, press center of each patty down until about ½ inch thick, creating slight divot.

**2**   Heat oil in 12-inch nonstick skillet over medium heat until just smoking. Transfer patties to skillet, divot side up, and cook until well browned on first side, 2 to 4 minutes. Flip patties, top with cheese, and continue to cook until browned on second side and meat registers 120 to 125 degrees (for medium-rare) or 130 to 135 degrees (for medium), 3 to 5 minutes. Transfer burgers to platter and let rest for 5 minutes.

**3**   Meanwhile, whisk mayonnaise, vinegar, sugar, pepper, and remaining ¼ teaspoon salt in medium bowl. Add coleslaw mix and toss to coat. Serve burgers on buns topped with coleslaw.

### Antoinette's Tip

Because of all the additions to the ground meat mixture, these burgers are a little more delicate than regular burger patties, so flip them gently. Pressing the divot into each patty keeps them from doming up and going meatball-shaped while they cook.

# Queso Dip

**Serves:** 6 to 8 (makes 1¾ cups)  ·  **Total time:** 10 minutes

*Texans are very serious about their queso dips. In fact, Ro-Tel, the canned combination of tomatoes and chiles, was created in Texas in the 1940s to help Texans make their beloved queso (and other dishes) more conveniently. Ro-Tel dip, with Velveeta and ground beef, became a mainstay, eventually spreading beyond Texas's borders. When I'm craving queso, I like to focus on the spicy cheese, so my updated version stays away from tomatoes and ground beef and uses two kinds of canned chiles: chipotles in adobo and green chiles. Both of these convenient, readily available ingredients add bold flavor, and the chipotles infuse the queso with a distinctive smokiness. My secret ingredient that sets this queso apart is evaporated milk. This pantry staple adds a concentrated creamy richness without overpowering the flavors of the cheese and chiles. Serve this with tortilla chips.*

1  (5-ounce) can evaporated milk

4  ounces Monterey Jack cheese, shredded (1 cup)

¼  cup canned chopped green chiles

2½  teaspoons minced canned chipotle chile in adobo sauce

¼  teaspoon garlic powder

Pinch table salt

Bring evaporated milk to simmer in small saucepan over medium heat. Off heat, add cheese, green chiles, chipotle, garlic powder, and salt, stirring until cheese is melted and well combined. Season with salt and pepper to taste. Transfer to bowl and serve.

## Pantry Pick

**Evaporated milk:** Like sweetened condensed milk, evaporated milk has had much of its water removed. Unlike sweetened condensed milk, evaporated milk has no sugar added, making it ideal for savory recipes. You can use evaporated milk as a substitute for regular milk by mixing equal quantities of water and evaporated milk.

# Cheesy Garlic Hawaiian Rolls

**Makes:** 12 rolls   ·   **Total time:** 30 minutes

*In true melting pot style, Hawaiian rolls got their start with Portuguese immigrants to the Hawaiian islands in the 19th century. The immigrants wanted to make their traditional sweet breads, and since sugar was expensive they used local ingredients, like the pineapple juice that is found in Hawaiian rolls. Now, I'm not sure who first realized that these rolls were delicious turned into garlic bread, but social media has most definitely discovered this secret! In case you don't know this—these fluffy, pillowy rolls are begging to be baked! To create the ultimate cheesy Hawaiian roll experience, I start by melting butter and infusing it with aromatic minced garlic, then stirring in chopped fresh parsley. Then I slash open the tops of the rolls and brush the butter all over them so that it sinks in deeply. Lots of versions either don't use cheese at all or add lots of shredded cheese; I opt for a small amount of deeply flavorful grated Pecorino Romano, which creates a delicate golden crust in the oven.*

6   tablespoons unsalted butter

3   garlic cloves, minced

¼   teaspoon table salt

2   tablespoons chopped fresh parsley

1   (12-ounce) package Hawaiian rolls

¼   cup grated Pecorino Romano cheese

**1**   Adjust oven rack to middle position and heat oven to 400 degrees. Melt butter in small saucepan over medium-low heat. Add garlic and salt and cook until fragrant, about 1 minute. Off heat, stir in parsley.

**2**   Remove rolls from packaging and place on aluminum foil–lined rimmed baking sheet, without separating rolls. Using serrated knife, make two 1-inch-deep slashes along top of each bun to form cross, then gently pull open bread at cuts to reveal interior of each roll. Brush melted butter mixture over top of rolls, being sure to brush into cuts in each roll, then sprinkle evenly with cheese. Bake until cheese is melted and rolls are well browned, 7 to 10 minutes. Serve.

# Lemon-Blueberry Dump Crumble

**Serves:** 10 to 12 · **Total time:** 1½ hours

*Dump cakes have been around for decades, and I remember my granny whipping them up all the time, creating warm and comforting treats that we kids couldn't resist. The premise of a dump cake, as the name suggests, is that the ingredients are simply dumped into the cake pan, with no mixing. A risk of this approach is that you can end up with uneven textures in the finished dessert. My updated version of this classic recipe solves the problem by turning the cake into a crumble. Combining the cake mix and melted butter in a bowl before scattering it on top of canned pie filling ensures an evenly crisp, crumbly topping without any dry clumps of cake mix in your dessert. I love the intense flavor combination of lemon and blueberry, but you could experiment with other flavor pairings. To add creaminess and a surprise tangy twist, I drizzle a cream cheese and lemon glaze over the warm baked crumble.*

1   (15.25-ounce) box lemon cake mix

8   tablespoons unsalted butter, melted

2   (21-ounce) cans blueberry pie filling

4   teaspoons lemon juice, divided

4   ounces cream cheese, softened

4   teaspoons milk

**1**   Adjust oven rack to middle position and heat oven to 350 degrees. Combine cake mix and melted butter in bowl, stirring with rubber spatula until clumps form and no dry mix remains.

**2**   Combine pie filling and 1 tablespoon lemon juice in 13- by 9-inch baking pan, then spread into even layer. Scatter cake mixture evenly over top, breaking up any clumps larger than a marble.

**3**   Bake until topping is golden brown, 40 to 45 minutes. Transfer pan to wire rack and let cool for 15 minutes. Whisk cream cheese, milk, and remaining 1 teaspoon lemon juice together in bowl, then drizzle decoratively over crumble. Let cool for 15 minutes longer. Serve warm.

## *Pantry Pick*

**Pie filling:** Keeping cans of pie filling on hand lets you make delectable desserts with little effort, since they are already sweetened and have a syrupy, cooked consistency. I also love canned pie filling in my Cherry-Bourbon Trifle (page 44).

# Nutritional Information for Our Recipes

To calculate the nutritional values of our recipes per serving, we used The Food Processor SQL by ESHA research. When using this program, we entered all the ingredients, using weights wherever possible. We also used our preferred brands in these analyses. Any ingredient listed as "optional" was excluded from the analyses. If there is a range in the serving size, we used the highest number of servings to calculate nutritional values. We did not include additional salt or pepper for food that's seasoned to taste.

| | Cal | Total Fat (g) | Sat Fat (g) | Chol (mg) | Sodium (mg) | Carbs (g) | Fiber (g) | Total Sugar (g) | Added Sugar (g) | Protein (g) |
|---|---|---|---|---|---|---|---|---|---|---|
| **Introduction** | | | | | | | | | | |
| **Pesto Sauce** | 110 | 11 | 2.5 | 5 | 100 | 0 | 0 | 0 | 0 | 2 |
| **Chimichurri** | 90 | 9 | 1.5 | 0 | 150 | 1 | 0 | 0 | 0 | 0 |
| **Pickled Vegetables** | 10 | 0 | 0 | 0 | 70 | 2 | 0 | 1 | 1 | 0 |
| **Berry Coulis** | 40 | 0 | 0 | 0 | 10 | 10 | 1 | 9 | 6 | 0 |
| **Maximize the Canned Aisle** | | | | | | | | | | |
| **Oysters Rockefeller Dip** | 180 | 17 | 11 | 65 | 160 | 3 | 0 | 1 | 0 | 4 |
| **Smoked Salmon Dip** | 160 | 11 | 6 | 90 | 560 | 3 | 0 | 1 | 0 | 13 |
| **Sriracha-Soy Salmon Sliders** | 480 | 20 | 3 | 150 | 1080 | 48 | 3 | 10 | 2 | 35 |
| **Linguine with Baby Clams** | 760 | 27 | 15 | 240 | 1660 | 91 | 2 | 8 | 0 | 40 |
| **Beer Brat Pasta** | 1280 | 80 | 32 | 195 | 2340 | 114 | 1 | 19 | 0 | 43 |
| **Weeknight Collard Greens** | 150 | 6 | 2 | 10 | 1320 | 14 | 5 | 6 | 4 | 7 |
| **Ginger-Miso Carrots** | 90 | 0 | 0 | 0 | 760 | 21 | 3 | 18 | 13 | 1 |
| **Tortellini Tomato Soup** | 410 | 13 | 5 | 30 | 1860 | 51 | 6 | 14 | 0 | 19 |
| **Sweet Potato Soufflé** | 190 | 6 | 3.5 | 65 | 75 | 31 | 1 | 23 | 6 | 5 |
| **No-Churn Sweet Potato Pie Ice Cream** | 320 | 20 | 13 | 65 | 125 | 32 | 1 | 29 | 9 | 4 |
| **Cherry-Bourbon Trifle** | 400 | 17 | 8 | 60 | 220 | 58 | 0 | 45 | 41 | 3 |
| **Make the Most of Pantry Ingredients** | | | | | | | | | | |
| **Hot Honey Mustard Slaw with Peanuts** | 110 | 4 | 0.5 | 0 | 350 | 16 | 3 | 7 | 4 | 4 |
| *Hot Honey Mustard–Peanut Dressing* | 35 | 1 | 0 | 0 | 300 | 5 | 0 | 4 | 4 | 1 |
| **Chopped Salad with Creamy Garlic Dressing** | 270 | 22 | 3 | 15 | 410 | 15 | 5 | 2 | 0 | 5 |
| *Creamy Garlic Dressing* | 190 | 20 | 3 | 10 | 110 | 1 | 0 | 0 | 0 | 1 |
| **Spicy Potato Salad with Honey-Chipotle Dressing** | 320 | 17 | 4.5 | 20 | 400 | 36 | 3 | 4 | 3 | 7 |
| *Honey-Chipotle Dressing* | 5 | 0.5 | 0 | 0 | 55 | 3 | 0 | 3 | 2 | 0 |

| | Cal | Total Fat (g) | Sat Fat (g) | Chol (mg) | Sodium (mg) | Carbs (g) | Fiber (g) | Total Sugar (g) | Added Sugar (g) | Protein (g) |
|---|---|---|---|---|---|---|---|---|---|---|
| **Make the Most of Pantry Ingredients (continued)** | | | | | | | | | | |
| Barbecue Sauce | 45 | 0 | 0 | 0 | 110 | 10 | 0 | 9 | 7 | 0 |
| Barbecue Spice Rub | 35 | 1 | 0 | 0 | 25 | 7 | 1 | 5 | 4 | 1 |
| Brown Sugar–Soy Sauce Stir-Fry | 210 | 7 | 1 | 0 | 1510 | 33 | 0 | 20 | 13 | 5 |
| Shrimp Caesar Wrap | 740 | 42 | 8 | 215 | 1580 | 55 | 1 | 5 | 0 | 31 |
| *Caesar Dressing* | 80 | 8 | 1.5 | 15 | 150 | 1 | 0 | 0 | 0 | 1 |
| Air-Fried Cod with Fried Food Sauce | 360 | 4 | 1 | 190 | 1540 | 29 | 1 | 1 | 0 | 48 |
| *Fried Food Sauce* | 280 | 28 | 4.5 | 15 | 1340 | 8 | 0 | 5 | 4 | 1 |
| Mustard Fried Branzino | 400 | 19 | 2 | 95 | 750 | 12 | 0 | 0 | 0 | 44 |
| The Perfect Steak | 540 | 35 | 12 | 145 | 690 | 3 | 1 | 0 | 0 | 50 |
| *All-Purpose Seasoning* | 30 | 0 | 0 | 0 | 5 | 7 | 1 | 0 | 0 | 1 |
| Lamb Meatballs in Gravy | 440 | 32 | 13 | 130 | 660 | 9 | 1 | 2 | 0 | 24 |
| Pork Chops, Stuffing, and Gravy | 840 | 54 | 23 | 160 | 1840 | 45 | 1 | 7 | 0 | 44 |
| Creamy Dijon-Rosemary Chicken | 340 | 23 | 10 | 105 | 840 | 7 | 1 | 2 | 0 | 21 |
| Air-Fried Chicken Tenders with Chipotle Mayo | 360 | 4.5 | 0 | 130 | 1470 | 25 | 1 | 8 | 7 | 55 |
| *Chipotle Mayo* | 100 | 10 | 1.5 | 5 | 135 | 0 | 0 | 0 | 0 | 0 |
| Curry-Braised Chicken Leg Quarters | 1610 | 130 | 60 | 510 | 1820 | 18 | 1 | 6 | 0 | 93 |
| Hot Pepper–Strawberry Wings | 330 | 17 | 5 | 135 | 540 | 20 | 0 | 16 | 0 | 24 |
| Air-Fried Game Day Wings | 270 | 17 | 5 | 135 | 1150 | 6 | 1 | 3 | 2 | 24 |
| **Reimagine Prepared Foods** | | | | | | | | | | |
| Hoisin Chicken Lettuce Wraps | 360 | 12 | 2.5 | 80 | 1140 | 28 | 2 | 15 | 0 | 34 |
| Barbecue Pulled Chicken Sandwiches | 490 | 12 | 3 | 60 | 1050 | 69 | 0 | 44 | 17 | 24 |
| Coconut Green Curry Chicken Noodle Soup | 490 | 19 | 12 | 70 | 1840 | 56 | 3 | 5 | 0 | 24 |
| White Chicken Chili | 350 | 19 | 9 | 115 | 1780 | 20 | 4 | 4 | 0 | 29 |
| Creamy Roasted Garlic and Chicken Pasta | 900 | 53 | 29 | 205 | 800 | 63 | 0 | 5 | 0 | 42 |
| *Air Fryer Roasted Garlic* | 30 | 0 | 0 | 0 | 25 | 5 | 0 | 0 | 0 | 1 |
| Mustard-Sesame Noodles | 250 | 7 | 0.5 | 85 | 1180 | 19 | 2 | 16 | 1 | 27 |
| Chicken Enchilada Bake | 560 | 25 | 14 | 110 | 1890 | 38 | 1 | 6 | 0 | 43 |
| Mini Chicken Pot Pies | 110 | 4.5 | 1 | 15 | 270 | 8 | 0 | 1 | 0 | 7 |
| Pesto Cheeseburgers | 1220 | 76 | 27 | 170 | 2100 | 76 | 2 | 8 | 1 | 56 |
| Air-Fried Pesto Chicken Roll-Ups | 360 | 23 | 7 | 90 | 560 | 11 | 0 | 2 | 0 | 28 |

| | Cal | Total Fat (g) | Sat Fat (g) | Chol (mg) | Sodium (mg) | Carbs (g) | Fiber (g) | Total Sugar (g) | Added Sugar (g) | Protein (g) |
|---|---|---|---|---|---|---|---|---|---|---|
| **Reimagine Prepared Foods (continued)** | | | | | | | | | | |
| Air-Fried Pesto Salmon | 530 | 36 | 8 | 100 | 600 | 10 | 0 | 2 | 0 | 39 |
| Pesto-Stuffed Mushrooms | 70 | 6 | 1.5 | 5 | 130 | 4 | 0 | 1 | 0 | 2 |
| Herbed Goat Cheese Scramble | 320 | 27 | 14 | 435 | 550 | 2 | 0 | 2 | 0 | 18 |
| Butternut Squash and Parmesan Soup | 160 | 6 | 3.5 | 15 | 920 | 21 | 3 | 6 | 0 | 6 |
| Chicken Gnocchi Soup | 390 | 21 | 8 | 80 | 1320 | 26 | 2 | 4 | 0 | 24 |
| Air-Fried Crispy Gnocchi with Artichokes | 350 | 21 | 8 | 30 | 1180 | 33 | 1 | 3 | 0 | 7 |
| Crispy Gnocchi with Roasted Red Pepper Sauce | 420 | 30 | 8 | 25 | 1120 | 34 | 1 | 6 | 0 | 5 |
| Weeknight Ravioli Lasagna | 350 | 17 | 8 | 110 | 1430 | 31 | 0 | 7 | 0 | 16 |
| Tortellini Salad | 390 | 25 | 5 | 20 | 970 | 30 | 0 | 1 | 0 | 9 |
| **Instant Pot Assets** | | | | | | | | | | |
| Instant Pot Baked Potato Soup | 450 | 25 | 12 | 60 | 1320 | 39 | 4 | 5 | 0 | 13 |
| Instant Pot Barbecue Burnt Ends | 860 | 32 | 10 | 235 | 1750 | 73 | 4 | 57 | 32 | 75 |
| Instant Pot Roast | 600 | 17 | 5 | 145 | 950 | 54 | 7 | 7 | 0 | 55 |
| Instant Pot Beef Ragu | 140 | 4.5 | 1.5 | 40 | 520 | 7 | 2 | 3 | 0 | 15 |
| Instant Pot Quesabirria Tacos | 550 | 21 | 9 | 135 | 1360 | 38 | 1 | 2 | 0 | 49 |
| Instant Pot Barbecue Ribs | 600 | 21 | 6 | 110 | 820 | 64 | 0 | 59 | 43 | 36 |
| Instant Pot Carolina-Style Pulled Pork | 470 | 31 | 12 | 140 | 2870 | 9 | 0 | 7 | 6 | 37 |
| Instant Pot Cajun-Inspired Shrimp and Rice | 360 | 4.5 | 0.5 | 105 | 1360 | 60 | 1 | 2 | 0 | 20 |
| Instant Pot Collard Greens | 180 | 9 | 2 | 45 | 1110 | 7 | 3 | 2 | 2 | 19 |
| **Oven and Done** | | | | | | | | | | |
| Oven-Roasted Smothered Chicken Thighs | 310 | 20 | 5 | 120 | 840 | 9 | 1 | 3 | 0 | 22 |
| Royce's Mini Chicken | 1250 | 96 | 38 | 515 | 550 | 21 | 3 | 14 | 13 | 75 |
| Not Your Mother's Meatloaf | 430 | 29 | 10 | 180 | 880 | 13 | 0 | 6 | 1 | 26 |
| Thyme-Mustard Crusted Pork Chops | 430 | 16 | 5 | 165 | 1730 | 3 | 1 | 1 | 0 | 65 |
| Oven-Roasted Lemon and Dill Branzino | 490 | 14 | 3 | 185 | 2630 | 1 | 0 | 0 | 0 | 84 |
| No-Boil Mushroom and Pea Penne | 1520 | 103 | 65 | 320 | 1770 | 108 | 3 | 20 | 0 | 32 |
| Bacon–Green Chile Quiche | 570 | 48 | 23 | 255 | 700 | 20 | 0 | 2 | 0 | 16 |
| Mini Carbonara Quiche Cups | 120 | 7 | 3.5 | 85 | 440 | 6 | 0 | 1 | 0 | 8 |
| Dijon-Lemon Roasted Cabbage Wedges | 150 | 7 | 1 | 0 | 910 | 15 | 6 | 8 | 0 | 3 |

| | Cal | Total Fat (g) | Sat Fat (g) | Chol (mg) | Sodium (mg) | Carbs (g) | Fiber (g) | Total Sugar (g) | Added Sugar (g) | Protein (g) |
|---|---|---|---|---|---|---|---|---|---|---|
| **Drinks and Snacks** | | | | | | | | | | |
| Pineapple-Peach Tea | 130 | 0 | 0 | 0 | 10 | 33 | 1 | 29 | 25 | 1 |
| Ginger-Orange Soda | 70 | 0 | 0 | 0 | 20 | 18 | 0 | 17 | 13 | 0 |
| Brazilian Lemonade | 150 | 2 | 1 | 5 | 35 | 34 | 2 | 28 | 13 | 2 |
| Secret Red Sangria | 300 | 0 | 0 | 0 | 15 | 43 | 0 | 40 | 26 | 1 |
| Goat Cheese–Stuffed Olives | 45 | 4.5 | 1 | 5 | 410 | 0 | 0 | 0 | 0 | 1 |
| Prosciutto–Goat Cheese Logs with Honey and Rosemary | 80 | 6 | 3 | 25 | 430 | 1 | 0 | 1 | 1 | 6 |
| Candied Prosciutto | 40 | 2 | 0 | 10 | 420 | 2 | 0 | 2 | 2 | 4 |
| Air-Fried Barbecue Chickpeas | 120 | 5 | 0.5 | 0 | 230 | 14 | 4 | 2 | 2 | 4 |
| Air-Fried Roasted Salsa | 15 | 0 | 0 | 0 | 440 | 3 | 1 | 2 | 0 | 1 |
| Crab Salad Pastry Puffs | 240 | 15 | 6 | 45 | 600 | 21 | 1 | 1 | 0 | 9 |
| Onion Jam and Goat Cheese Flatbread | 200 | 7 | 2.5 | 15 | 630 | 23 | 0 | 3 | 1 | 7 |
| Candied Walnuts | 240 | 16 | 1.5 | 0 | 80 | 22 | 2 | 19 | 19 | 4 |
| Sparkling Whipped Cream Dip with Berries | 120 | 11 | 7 | 35 | 25 | 4 | 0 | 4 | 3 | 1 |
| Sweet Potato Pie Dip | 90 | 2.5 | 1.5 | 10 | 55 | 16 | 1 | 11 | 3 | 2 |
| Brown Sugar Caramel Sauce | 130 | 8 | 5 | 25 | 25 | 13 | 0 | 13 | 13 | 0 |
| **Mostly Homemade Classics, Updated** | | | | | | | | | | |
| Overnight Breakfast Casserole | 240 | 16 | 7 | 125 | 859 | 12 | 9 | 2 | 9 | 14 |
| Strawberry-Hoisin Meatballs | 220 | 13 | 5 | 25 | 520 | 19 | 1 | 13 | 0 | 7 |
| Sausage Balls with Lime-Cilantro Dipping Sauce | 340 | 25 | 13 | 75 | 860 | 13 | 0 | 2 | 0 | 16 |
| Pigs on a Blanket | 340 | 21 | 9 | 15 | 570 | 37 | 1 | 8 | 2 | 9 |
| Barbecue Chicken Leg Quarters | 1220 | 88 | 24 | 510 | 2220 | 11 | 1 | 7 | 7 | 89 |
| Carolina-Style Cheeseburgers | 730 | 50 | 16 | 115 | 1420 | 34 | 2 | 11 | 3 | 33 |
| Queso Dip | 160 | 11 | 7 | 35 | 300 | 4 | 0 | 4 | 0 | 9 |
| Cheesy Garlic Hawaiian Rolls | 140 | 7 | 4 | 15 | 179 | 15 | 0 | 4 | 0 | 3 |
| Lemon-Blueberry Dump Crumble | 420 | 12 | 8 | 30 | 310 | 75 | 0 | 54 | 2 | 2 |

# Conversions and Equivalents

Some say cooking is a science and an art. We would say that geography has a hand in it, too. Flours and sugars manufactured in the United Kingdom and elsewhere will feel and taste different from those manufactured in the United States. So we cannot promise that the loaf of bread you bake in Canada or England will taste the same as a loaf baked in the States, but we can offer guidelines for converting weights and measures. We also recommend that you rely on your instincts when making our recipes. Refer to the visual cues provided. If the dough hasn't "come together in a ball" as described, you may need to add more flour—even if the recipe doesn't tell you to. You be the judge.

The recipes in this book were developed using standard U.S. measures following U.S. government guidelines. The charts below offer equivalents for U.S. and metric measures. All conversions are approximate and have been rounded up or down to the nearest whole number.

*example:*
1 teaspoon = 4.9292 milliliters, rounded up to 5 milliliters
1 ounce =   28.3495 grams, rounded down to 28 grams

## Volume Conversions

| U.S. | metric |
|---|---|
| 1 teaspoon | 5 milliliters |
| 2 teaspoons | 10 milliliters |
| 1 tablespoon | 15 milliliters |
| 2 tablespoons | 30 milliliters |
| ¼ cup | 59 milliliters |
| ⅓ cup | 79 milliliters |
| ½ cup | 118 milliliters |
| ¾ cup | 177 milliliters |
| 1 cup | 237 milliliters |
| 1¼ cups | 296 milliliters |
| 1½ cups | 355 milliliters |
| 2 cups (1 pint) | 473 milliliters |
| 2½ cups | 591 milliliters |
| 3 cups | 710 milliliters |
| 4 cups (1 quart) | 0.946 liter |
| 1.06 quarts | 1 liter |
| 4 quarts (1 gallon) | 3.8 liters |

## Weight Conversions

| ounces | grams |
|---|---|
| ½ | 14 |
| ¾ | 21 |
| 1 | 28 |
| 1½ | 43 |
| 2 | 57 |
| 2½ | 71 |
| 3 | 85 |
| 3½ | 99 |
| 4 | 113 |
| 4½ | 128 |
| 5 | 142 |
| 6 | 170 |
| 7 | 198 |
| 8 | 227 |
| 9 | 255 |
| 10 | 283 |
| 12 | 340 |
| 16 (1 pound) | 454 |

## Conversions for Common Baking Ingredients

Baking is an exacting science. Because measuring by weight is far more accurate than measuring by volume, and thus more likely to produce reliable results, in our recipes we provide ounce measures in addition to cup measures for many ingredients. Refer to the chart below to convert these measures into grams.

| ingredient | ounces | grams |
|---|---|---|
| **flour** | | |
| 1 cup all-purpose flour* | 5 | 142 |
| 1 cup cake flour | 4 | 113 |
| 1 cup whole-wheat flour | 5½ | 156 |
| **sugar** | | |
| 1 cup granulated (white) sugar | 7 | 198 |
| 1 cup packed brown sugar (light or dark) | 7 | 198 |
| 1 cup confectioners' sugar | 4 | 113 |
| **cocoa powder** | | |
| 1 cup cocoa powder | 3 | 85 |
| **butter†** | | |
| 4 tablespoons (½ stick or ¼ cup) | 2 | 57 |
| 8 tablespoons (1 stick or ½ cup) | 4 | 113 |
| 16 tablespoons (2 sticks or 1 cup) | 8 | 227 |

\* U.S. all-purpose flour, the most frequently used flour in this book, does not contain leaveners, as some European flours do. These leavened flours are called self-rising or self-raising. If you are using self-rising flour, take this into consideration before adding leaveners to a recipe.

† In the United States, butter is sold both salted and unsalted. We generally recommend unsalted butter. If you are using salted butter, take this into consideration before adding salt to a recipe.

## Oven Temperatures

| fahrenheit | celsius | gas mark |
|---|---|---|
| 225 | 105 | ¼ |
| 250 | 120 | ½ |
| 275 | 135 | 1 |
| 300 | 150 | 2 |
| 325 | 165 | 3 |
| 350 | 180 | 4 |
| 375 | 190 | 5 |
| 400 | 200 | 6 |
| 425 | 220 | 7 |
| 450 | 230 | 8 |
| 475 | 245 | 9 |

## Converting Temperatures from an Instant-Read Thermometer

We include doneness temperatures in many of the recipes in this book. We recommend an instant-read thermometer for the job. Refer to the table above to convert Fahrenheit degrees to Celsius. Or, for temperatures not represented in the chart, use this simple formula:

Subtract 32 degrees from the Fahrenheit reading, then divide the result by 1.8 to find the Celsius reading.

*example:*
"Roast chicken until thighs register 175 degrees."

*to convert:*
175°F − 32 = 143°
143° ÷ 1.8 = 79.44°C, rounded down to 79°C

# Index

Note: Page references in *italics* indicate photographs.

# O

# P